JOHN WIMBER'S
TEACHING
ON
THE *GIFT* AND *GIFTS*
OF THE HOLY SPIRIT

Øyvind Nerheim & Derek Morphew

PUBLICATION DETAILS

Vineyard International Publishing
84 Starke Road, Bergvliet, 7945, South Africa

ISBN: 9798687497480

LIST OF ABBREVIATIONS

NASB	New American Standard Version
NB11	Bibelen, 2011 edition, Det norske Bibelselskap
NB88	Norsk Bibel, 1988 edition
NIDNTT	New International Dictionary of New Testament Theology
NIV	New International Version
KNT	N. T. Wright, The Kingdom New Testament
VCF	Vineyard Christian Fellowship
AVC	The Association of Vineyard Churches
VMI	Vineyard Ministries International

LIST OF TABLES AND DIAGRAMS

TABLE OF CONTENTS

INTRODUCTION

INTRODUCING JOHN WIMBER

John Wimber was the first International Director of the Vineyard movement and had a formative influence on renewal movements in England among Anglican churches, particularly New Wine, launched from St. Andrews', Chorleywood, and Holy Trinity Brompton. Apart from these church groupings he had a remarkably far-reaching influence on the international Christian community of almost every denomination.

During his career he was a Quaker pastor, a lecturer in the Fuller Theological Seminary School of World Missions, a Church Growth consultant, founding pastor of the *Anaheim Vineyard Christian Fellowship,* a well-known author (his best known works being *Power Healing* and *Power Evangelism*), an international conference speaker and a father figure to many church leaders in many countries, who regarded him as their primary mentor. *Christianity Today* magazine featured him in one of its cover stories, naming him as one of the leading Christian figures of the last century.

HIS INNOVATIVE THEOLOGICAL CONTRIBUTIONS

Wimber's contribution to fresh theological thinking was more diverse than many are aware of. As a result of his best-known publications, he is usually associated with power healing and power evangelism. But there was more to Wimber than that. Here are some of his other contributions, each of them leading to fresh insights and practices.

Since he was a church growth consultant, his teaching on church planting was a major influence on his contemporaries and led to many pioneers launching church plants, not only in the United States, but all over the world. This resource is now available in *John Wimber's Teaching on*

Church Planting (2020).[1]

His total theological journey, including his discovery of the kingdom of God and its implications, have been well documented by Doug Erickson in *Living the Future: The Kingdom of God and the Holy Spirit in the Vineyard Movement* (2016) [2] and described by Alexander Venter as a philosophy of ministry in *Doing Church* (2000).[3] There are two aspects of this larger picture which this book will explore further.

The gift, or empowering of the Holy Spirit

Wimber would habitually teach on the relationship between the Vineyard and Pentecostalism using this table.

Pentecostal—Vineyard Relationship: Wimber's diagram		
	Theology	Practice
Conservative Evangelical	X	
Pentecostal		X

While this is true as a generalization, it does require some nuancing. By being Pentecostal in practice, Wimber affirmed his commitment to continuationism, or the repudiation of cessationism. The gifts of the Holy Spirit did not cease after the apostolic age, continued to be manifest at different levels of intensity throughout the history of the church, and were to be a vital element in ministry today. His works on power healing and power evangelism were based on this assumption.

By placing the theological position of the Vineyard within evangelicalism, Wimber affirmed what has generally been described as third-wave evangelicalism. More specifically, this implied that he did not affirm the two classic Pentecostal doctrines of subsequence and evidence. "Subsequence" refers to the teaching that the baptism in the Holy Spirit is an experience subsequent to conversion and regeneration, and that this is normative. "Evidence" refers to the teaching that speaking in tongues is the

---

[1]Derek Morphew, *John Wimber's Teaching on Church Planting*, Cape Town: Vineyard International Publishing, 2020.

[2]Douglas Erickson, *The Spirit and the Kingdom*, Doctoral Dissertation submitted to Marquette University, 2015; *Living the Future: The Kingdom of God and the Holy Spirit in the Vineyard Movement,* 2016.

[3]Alexander Venter, *Doing Church,* 2000.

indispensable sign of having been baptised in the Holy Spirit.

While the latter is a true reflection of Wimber's teaching, the former is not quite. Wimber fully appreciated the Pauline letters—for instance teaching an expository series on Ephesians—but his primary works on power healing and power evangelism are premised on the theology of Luke-Acts. His slogan, "doing the stuff" expressed his conviction that ministry today should be modeled on the ministry of Jesus in the gospels. We should announce and demonstrate the kingdom of God, doing the words and works of Jesus, as he did. We know this, because Luke's two volumes draw a deliberate parallel between the ministry of Jesus in the gospels and the ministry of the early church in Acts.

If one considers this in the light or recent theological trends, is a case of narrative theology. God's primary vehicle for communicating his word to us is the grand narrative of Scripture. This led Wimber to his more nuanced approach to the empowering of the Spirit. He did not follow the typical conservative evangelical line, that we should only base our doctrines on didactic portions of Scripture, like the Pauline letters and Jesus' sermon on the mount, and not on narrative portions of Scripture. Wimber chose to base his views on the empowering or reception of the Spirit in Pauline theology *and* the theology of Luke-Acts. He was one of the first to argue that what Paul meant by the phrase "baptism in the Spirit" and what Luke meant by that phrase were not the same. Therefore, while conservative evangelicals have imposed Paul's meaning onto Luke, and Pentecostals have imposed Luke's meaning onto Paul, Wimber held to a more nuanced view that affirmed both. This enabled him to come to a more flexible understanding of the reception or empowering of the Spirit.

In this sense Wimber's teaching breaks out from the century old disagreement between conservative evangelicals and Pentecostals. This is one of his innovative contributions. Derek Morphew will explore this aspect of Wimber's contribution in Part One.

The gifts of the Holy Spirit

The experience of being empowered by the Spirit leads directly to the Christian disciple operating in the gifts of the Spirit. Here again Wimber made a fresh contribution. Another one of his slogans articulates his approach: "we all get to play." He was concerned that elements within the Pentecostal tradition had effectively produced a culture of anointed

9

"superstars" who moved effectively in the charismatic gifts, making the general Christian disciple an observer more than a participant. While he put some of this down to ministry models, often saying that "models rule", he also discerned that the more fundamental issue was the theology of the charismatic gifts. This led to his notion of "situational" versus "static" gifts of the Spirit and to his metaphor of the gifts as "the dancing hand of God."

Øyvind Nerheim will explore this aspect of Wimber's teaching in Part Two.

THE TWO AUTHORS

Derek Morphew

Derek Morphew was educated at Michaelhouse High School in Natal, South Africa, where he was converted to Christ through the ministry of Michael Cassidy, a well-known South African Evangelist. He then did his theological training at Rhodes University, where he majored in Biblical Studies and Systematic Theology, after which he obtained his PhD in the field of New Testament Studies at the University of Cape Town.

His career has gone through various stages, first as pastor and church planter, then as coach and overseer to pastors and churches, then as developer of educational systems and textbook content, and now as author and theological consultant. He has been a conference and seminar speaker for most of his career, speaking and teaching in more than twenty countries.

Øyvind Nerheim

Øyvind Nerheim is in a diakonal trust as a project leader for digitalication and construction and real estate development. He has also worked as an administrator at Oslo Vinyard, and has been a small group leader, a sound guy and has been leading a change prosess for the church. Sound and light ministry has been his main area of service in the church. He and his wife Ellen have five kids between eleven and twenty-one. They live in Nittedal close to Oslo.

His masters thesis, *Spiritual Gifts: A dynamic view based on John Wimber* was submitted to the Norwegian School of Theology in 2005. It is the most comprehensive and well researched text on Wimber's teaching on the gifts of the Spirit.

Previously he completed a Master's thesis in Intercultural Studies at Fuller Theological Seminary, Pasadena, Los Angeles, CA, namely *Church Conflict: The Pastoral Overseer's Authority Base in a Relationship Based Church Movement Like the Vineyard.*

PART ONE: THE GIFT OF THE SPIRIT

By Derek Morphew

It would be misleading to say that Part One is all based on Wimber's teaching on this topic. It begins with Wimber's fresh contribution, and then makes use of more recent trends in theology to further develop and support his position. Hopefully, it builds on his formative insights and does not distort them. These further explorations are based on a chapter in Derek Morphew's publication: *Demonstrating the Kingdom* (2019)[4] and a dialogue with Thomas Lyons doctoral dissertation.[5]

---

[4]Derek Morphew, *Demonstrating the Kingdom*, Cape Town: Vineyard International Publishing, 2019.

[5]Thomas Lyons, *Revisiting The Riddle In Samaria: A Social-Scientific Investigation Of Spirit Reception In Luke-Acts In Historical Perspective*, Doctoral Dissertation submitted to Asbury Theological Seminar, February 2020.

AVOIDING PARALYSIS

THE COMMAND OF JESUS

During his resurrection encounters with his disciples, Jesus gave this command:

> Do not leave Jerusalem, but wait for the gift my Father promised, which you have heard me speak about. For John baptized with water, but in a few days, you will be baptized with the Holy Spirit (Acts 1:4–5).

He told them,

> You will receive power when the Holy Spirit comes on you; and you will be my witnesses in Jerusalem, and in all Judea and Samaria, and to the ends of the earth (Acts 1:8).

They obeyed his command. They did not simply wait, passively, but they engaged in active and purposeful prayer. Gathered in the upper room,

> They all joined together constantly in prayer, along with the women and Mary the mother of Jesus, and with his brothers (Acts 1:14).

Many days later, "When the day of Pentecost came," they were still "all together in one place" (Acts 2:1).

One wonders what they prayed. Since Jesus told them to wait for the Holy Spirit to come upon them, one would assume their prayer was, "Lord, let your Holy Spirit come on us, as you have promised" or words to that effect. One often hears people say they cannot find a clear prayer in Scripture saying, "Come Holy Spirit" but it does not take a lot of deduction to conclude that this was basically what they were praying for.[6] This was a prolonged, purposeful, specific type of praying, by a community in unison: all together, for the Holy Spirit to come.

---

[6] Jesus also tells us the Father will give the Holy Spirit to those who ask (Luke 11:13).

This command, recorded in Acts 1, is also given in Luke 24:49,

> I am going to send you what my Father has promised; but stay in the city until you have been clothed with power from on high.

Clearly Jesus did not envision the church being able to fulfil its missional task without this Holy Spirit empowering. Clearly the first disciples took him seriously and prayed, earnestly, for days, for the promise to be fulfilled. From the subsequent story of Acts, it is also clear that the mission of the church was based on the empowering they did receive. There is no other explanation for the successful witness, preaching, signs and wonders, evangelism, growth, and church planting of the early church.

The question we address here is: how do we obey this command today, and how do we pray in this way?

Despite the crucial nature of this question, there is a danger that we will remain paralysed by arguments about how and when the Holy Spirit comes, and what is meant by the term "baptism in the Holy Spirit." Our goal is to get to talk about how we can minister the empowering of the Spirit, and how we can seek, or "wait" for it, just as they did. But to get there, we need to remove the paralysis.

AVOIDING PARALYSIS: WIMBER'S BOTH/AND

It is well known that conservative evangelicals and Pentecostals do not agree on this at all. Where then do we stand?

In this regard, John Wimber was remarkably ahead of his time. In *Power Evangelism* he has a chapter called "Empowered by the Holy Spirit" where he argues for a both/and position.[7] Essentially, he did not agree with either of the opposing sides.

He notes that arguments about the baptism in the Holy Spirit usually come down to labels.[8] He then goes on to state that

> Paul and Luke used the term "baptism in the Holy Spirit" differently. Paul used it to mean an initial action of the Holy Spirt that incorporates the individual into the body of Christ at conversion (especially see 1 Corinthians 12:13). Luke used it to mean an endowment with power for effective witness and service, an

---

[7] John Wimber, *Power Evangelism,* London: Hodder and Stoughton, 1986, 132–146.
[8] Ibid., 140.

experience that can be repeated.[9]

He then suggests that if we follow Paul, we would talk about being born again followed by various "fillings", while if we follow Luke, there is "warrant in using 'being baptised with the Holy Spirit'" for a distinct empowering experience.[10] Wimber believed that "There is in Scripture no discernible pattern or formula for how the Spirit falls on us."[11] In another place he says,

> It is a simple fact: God has a work of conversion; God has a work of empowerment. It can occur simultaneously, it can occur sequentially, it can occur with a long intermission in between the two, or it can occur in a short period of time, but the bottom line is that it needs to occur. It is the infilling empowering of the church and we need it in order to accommodate the work of God. Conversion is truly a baptism in the Holy Spirit. There is no reason that we cannot use baptism to refer to subsequent fillings of the Spirit as well, and I do.[12]

There is the both/and.

What has happened since Wimber wrote these words?

His far sightedness, along with those who advised him, has merely been underlined. On the one hand all sorts of work has been done on Paul,[13] but more significantly recent theological disciplines[14] have made great strides on Luke as a theologian and the importance of narrative sections of Scripture as a basis for theology.[15] This development has seriously undermined

---

[9]Ibid., 141.

[10]Ibid.

[11]Cited in Doug Erickson, *Living the Future,* 153, from John Wimber, *Power Points,* New York: Harper Collins, 1991, 137.

[12]Cited in Doug Erickson, *Living the Future,* 121, from John Wimber, *Baptism in the Spirit,* Audio Resource available from Wimber.org, 1991.

[13]For a good summary of the so-called "New Perspective" on Paul, see Magnus Zetterholm, *Approaches to Paul: A Students Guide to Recent Scholarship,* Minneapolis: Fortress Press, 2009.

[14]These include biblical theology, redaction criticism and narrative criticism. I refer to this in Derek Morphew, *The Mission of the Kingdom, the Theology of Luke-Acts,* Cape Town: Vineyard International Publishing, 2011, 9–18 and *The Kingdom Reformation,* Cape Town: Vineyard International Publishing, 2020, 360-377.

[15]Almost all the writings of N.T. Wright, including those under his popular name Tom Wright, are excellent examples of narrative theology.

some early conservative evangelical statements. For instance, John Stott argued that

> this revelation of the purpose of God in Scripture should be sought primarily in its *didactic* rather than its *descriptive* parts. More precisely, we should look for it in the teaching of Jesus, and in the sermons and writings of the apostles, rather than in the purely narrative portions of the Acts.[16]

But a little thought will show how dubious this statement is. Vast sections of the bible are narrative ("descriptive"). Narrative is found in the Pentateuch, in the Old Testament historical books, and most importantly, large sections of the gospels, particularly Mark, who has proportionately less teaching and much more story telling. Recent studies show how carefully designed both Mark and Luke–Acts are, and how the authors have embedded their theology, or teaching, in their narrative structure. Stott's idea also repudiates Paul's statement that "all Scripture is God-breathed and is useful for teaching" (2 Timothy 3:16).[17]

Another development since Wimber has been to clarify how biblical words have meanings in context.[18] We cannot import the meaning of a word or phrase used by one biblical author and impose it on another biblical author. Words have meanings in sentences, sentences have meanings in paragraphs, paragraphs have meanings in the flow, or argument of a text, and those meanings have a context in the larger writings of a particular author or corpus (books associated with same author).[19] Further, the New Testament contains three major sectors, each of which take up a significant percentage of the total, the writings of Paul (roughly 25%), the writings of Luke (roughly 25%) and John or Johannine writings (roughly 33%). If we believe in the sovereignty of God in the formation of the New Testament canon, then we must receive Luke as a major contributor, along with Paul. Therefore, to attempt to read Paul's use of language about the Spirit

---

[16]John Stott, *Baptism and Fullness: The Work of the Holy Spirit Today*, Downers Grove, IVP, 2006, 21.

[17]This view has been decisively answered by Roger Stronstad in *The Charismatic Theology of St. Luke: Trajectories from the Old Testament to Luke-Acts*, Grand Rapids, Baker, 2012, 7–14.

[18]One of the formative thinkers was James Barr.

[19]I cover this in Derek Morphew, *Biblical Interpretation 101, Historic Rules for Reading the Bible*, Cape Town, Vineyard International Publishing, 2012, 42–65.

into Luke's use of language is to transgress some fundamental rules of biblical interpretation.[20]

Many conservative evangelical writers, and surprisingly, some charismatic ones, still engage in such dubious arguments.[21]

Further, we can now rely on some respected New Testament scholars in the Pentecostal and charismatic tradition that have underlined Wimber's views, especially on the fact that Paul and Luke use their language differently.[22]

Peter David's, author of various commentaries for the *New*

---

[20]A classic case would be to take what John means when he writes, "the word became flesh" in John 1 and impose it on what Paul means in Romans 7:18 when he writes "I know that good itself does not dwell in me, that is, in my sinful nature" (literally "flesh"). In the former "flesh" means full human bodily existence, in the latter it means fallen or sinful human nature.

[21]For instance, I was quite surprised to find that Simon Ponsonby, such an excellent teacher, remains within this framework. He clearly reads Paul into Luke, in *More*, Eastbourne: Kingsway, 2009, 149–171. My issue with Simon's treatment is not so much what he says, since there is so much good material, but what he leaves out. He does not refer at all to recent developments in biblical theology or narrative criticism, or to language use by different biblical writers, or the way Luke draws on the Old Testament language and theology of the Spirit, or the distinction between commissioning and empowering, or the notion of Pentecost as succession narrative, or to conceptions of the coming of the Spirit in Second Temple Jewish literature.

A key development in the last seventy years is Jesus Research, or the rediscovery of Jesus in the context of Second Temple Judaism. This has led to a rediscovery of the central kingdom mission and message of Jesus. As a result, where historically Protestants have begun with Paul, and then wearing Pauline lenses, have read the gospels and Acts, we now work in reverse. We begin with Jesus in the gospels, then wearing kingdom lenses, we read Paul. This makes the reading of Pauline language into Luke-Acts more questionable than in the past. Many Protestant evangelical scholars who read Paul into Luke are unconscious of their bias, or perhaps, how dated their approach is. This is explored more fully in *The Kingdom Reformation*, 402-472.

[22]One of the earliest scholars to point this out was Howard M. Ervin. Commenting on Paul's use of "baptism in the Spirit" he writes, "It is faulty methodology, however, to read this usage back into the book of Acts, and, on this basis, to assert that Jesus (and Peter) used this phrase with exactly the same meaning. They apparently did not, as a critical comparison demonstrates", *These Are Not Drunken as Ye Suppose,* Plainfield: Logos International, 1968, 47. He then goes on to describe how language works: "it must be pointed out that such ambiguities are inherent in language usages, and that it is the task of exegesis to unravel such equivocal terminology…The context is decisive for the final meaning of any word, or phrase, and not the dictionary definition", 47.

17

International Commentary series, writes,

> Each New Testament writer uses 'baptism' in his own way. In ritual contexts baptism indicates ritual union, ritual overwhelming, or ritual cleansing. Luke, as we have seen, refers to overwhelming as a means to empowering. Peter in 1 Peter 3:18–22 refers to ritual cleansing. Paul in Romans 6 seems to have overtones of both overwhelming (i.e. death) and union (union with Christ in his death and resurrection). Yet in 1 Corinthians 12 the aspect of union is the most prominent without any reference to death. This is truly a very flexible metaphor; context alone can determine what an author means by it. It must not be pre-defined by how another author…uses it.[23]

Then there is the massive four volume commentary on Acts by Craig Keener.[24] He similarly agrees that Paul and Luke use their language differently. In Luke, baptism in the Spirit refers to "his own special emphasis in his narrative" which "usually lies on the more particular dimension of empowering for service".[25]

> Luke allows that, in some cases, people experienced this prophetic-empowerment dimension shortly after, or (from a different perspective) as a later stage in their conversion process.[26]

Luke also uses the term "gift of the Spirit" differently.

> Surveying the context of the references in Paul and (for the most part) John suggests that the expression refers to conversion, which initiates a person into the continuing life by the Spirit; by contrast, the context of the passages in Acts suggests especially prophetic

---

[23]Peter Davids, *The Ministry of the Kingdom, Part 2,* unpublished manuscript that was part of the Vineyard Bible Institute curriculum.

[24]As well as his more popular book, Craig Keener, *Gift and Giver, the Holy Spirit for Today,* Baker Academic, 2001.

[25]Craig Keener, *Acts, An Exegetical Commentary, Volume 1,* Grand Rapids: Baker, 2012, 680.

[26]Keener, *Acts, Volume 1,* 681. He comments that "Whereas those who deny subsequence often dismiss advocates of subsequence as biased, the assumption that Luke must employ phrases in the same manner as Paul seems to me to be a frequent bias in the argument against subsequence in Luke's narratives," note 294.

empowerment.[27]

Commenting on the story of the Samaritan Pentecost, he says, "it would be sufficient to call into question the frequent practise of assuming that we understand Luke's pneumatology fully by reading into it Paul's".[28] "Luke probably uses the expression 'receiving the Spirit' differently from Paul, because his emphasis differs, focusing on empowerment more than on new life."[29]

---

[27]Ibid., 986.
[28]Keener, *Acts, Volume 2*, 1522.
[29]Ibid., 1524.

TWO VIEWS OF THE SPIRIT'S WORK

These somewhat technical details lead us to face the issue head on. We have two views about the work of the Spirit in the believer. They do not contradict each other at all, but they witness to more than one work of the Spirit.

For Paul, to be converted and incorporated into Christ is to be baptised in the Holy Spirit (1 Corinthians 12:13).[30] To be a Christian is to have the Spirit living in you. If you do not have the Spirit, you cannot be a Christian (Romans 8:9–11). This receiving of the Spirit happens when we are regenerated or born again (Titus 3:4–7).[31] The roots of Paul's view of the Spirit

---

[30]"For we were all baptized by one Spirit so as to form one body— whether Jews or Gentiles, slave or free— and we were all given the one Spirit to drink." Notice how this is the common experience of *all* baptized Christians.

The traditional Pentecostal reply to the evangelical position is to speak of the subject, the baptiser, and the element, to make Paul speak about the repentant sinner (subject) being baptized by the Spirit into the body of Christ (the element) in Corinthians; while Pentecost describes a baptism of the believer (subject) by Christ into the Holy Spirit (the element). This is the view taken for instance by L. Thomas Holdcroft, *The Holy Spirit, A Pentecostal Interpretation*, Springfield: Gospel Publishing House, 1979, 127–133. The problem is that prepositions in *koine* Greek do not work like this. The preposition ἐν (*en*) means both in (the element) and by (instrumental) depending on the context, but we can never be certain which way to take it. We cannot base an argument on the Greek preposition. The danger of this is well explained in an appendix in the *NIDNTT*, Volume 3, 1171–1215 on "Prepositions and Theology in the Greek New Testament." The most we can say from the way it is used here is that the result is that we are incorporated into the body of Christ. The use of prepositions is a weak argument. It is much better to work on the different language game of each biblical writer, not just on the phrase "baptism in the Spirit" but their whole range of terms and how they are used in context.

[31]"But when the kindness and love of God our Savior appeared, he saved us, not because of righteous things we had done, but because of his mercy. He saved us through the washing of rebirth and renewal by the Holy Spirit, whom he poured out on us generously through Jesus Christ our Savior, so that, having been justified by his grace, we might become heirs having the hope of eternal life" (Titus 3:4–7). Notice the repeated use of being "saved" and the blending of justification by grace, the rebirth and renewal by the Holy Spirit "poured

are to be found in Ezekiel's prophecy about the heart purified by the Spirit (Ezekiel 11:19–20; 36:25–29). His emphasis is more on the regenerating and sanctifying work of the Spirit than on the empowering work of the Spirit.

Another interesting aspect is that what is meant by the coming of the kingdom of God in the synoptic gospels is translated into life in the Spirit in Paul's writings.[32] The new life of entering the kingdom is life in the Spirit (2 Corinthians 3:3–6). It is the Spirit that brings righteousness and justification (1 Corinthians 6:11; Romans 9:10; 14:17; Galatians 3:14; 5:5). It is the Holy Spirit that brings us sonship (Romans 9:14–15, 23; Galatians 4:6).

For Luke, a cluster of terms describe what is essentially a prophetic, empowering work of the Spirit: the promise of the Father (Luke 24:49; Acts 1:4; 2:33), being clothed with power (Luke 24:49), being baptised with or in the Holy Spirit (Acts 1:5), receiving power when the Holy Spirit comes on you (Acts 1:8), being filled with the Holy Spirit (Acts 2:4) and receiving the Holy Spirit (Acts 8:17; 10:47). Generally, this does not describe the work of the Spirit in conversion and regeneration.

These two views of the work of the Spirit have led to the longstanding argument about "subsequence" versus a "simultaneous" reception of the Spirit. The Pentecostals, using Acts, teach that the baptism in the Spirit is *subsequent* to conversion. The evangelicals, following Paul, and reading Paul into the narrative of Acts, teach that receiving the Spirit is *simultaneous* with conversion.[33]

How should we think about these two views? Here our kingdom of God lenses come into operation.

KINGDOM LENSES

Viewed through the lenses of the kingdom, the either/or becomes less problematic, enabling us to fully embrace the both/and. The kingdom is the inbreaking of the powers of the coming age, or the age to come, into

---

out" on all in the same context.

[32]This has been clearly presented by Youngmo Cho, *Spirit and Kingdom in the Writings of Luke and Paul,* Eugene: Wipf and Stock, 2005, 52–109.

[33]We should note that Reformed Protestant evangelicals are rather isolated in their view. The Church Fathers, the Catholic and Anglican high church tradition, Methodism and the holiness movement, and the Pentecostals, all see some sort of subsequence.

this age, in Jesus and in Pentecost. If we ask *when* this inbreaking occurred, we find that a whole series of events were the arrival of the kingdom. We can think of at least seven ways in which the kingdom came.

1. In Luke 1–2 the dawning of the new age is announced. A whole series of prophetic phenomena populate the birth narrative. Zechariah receives an angelic revelation about his son, John, who will be filled with the Spirit from his birth. Mary is told that the Son of David will be born in her through the Holy Spirit. When Elizabeth and Mary met, "the baby leaped in her womb, and Elizabeth was filled with the Holy Spirit" (Luke 1:41). Both Mary and Zechariah break out into prophetic utterance, as does the old man Simeon. In his song, Zechariah thanks God for the "rising sun" dawning on them (Luke 2:78). The angels celebrate the enormity of the event of Christ's birth (2:8–14). All this is eschatological language about the new era of the kingdom. We can truly affirm that the kingdom began to arrive from the birth of Jesus.

2. The baptism of Jesus marks the moment when the messianic anointing comes on him (Matthew 3:16–17; Mark 1:9–11; Luke 3:21–22). Luke describes how Jesus was full of the Spirit from that moment on (Luke 4:1) and how after his victory over the devil he returned "in the power of the Spirit" to begin his ministry of healing and liberation (Luke 4:14). We could say that the messianic era truly began from the baptism and anointing of the Spirit on Jesus.

3. Another key turning point was the transition between John the Baptist and Jesus. John is viewed as the greatest of the Old Testament prophets, while with Jesus the new era begins (Mark 1:14–15).

> Truly I tell you, among those born of women there has not risen anyone greater than John the Baptist; yet whoever is least in the kingdom of heaven is greater than he. From the days of John the Baptist until now, the kingdom of heaven has been subjected to violence,[34] and violent people have been raiding it. For all the Prophets and the Law prophesied until John. And if you are willing to accept it, he is the Elijah who

---

[34]Or "has been coming violently" (NRSV footnote). N. T. Wright, KNT, translates "the kingdom of heaven has been forcing its way in – and the men of force are trying to grab it!"

was to come. Whoever has ears, let them hear (Matthew 11:11–15).

Luke makes a similar statement (Luke 16:16).

> The Law and the Prophets were proclaimed until John. Since that time, the good news of the kingdom of God is being preached, and everyone is forcing their way into it.[35]

The key phrases "From the days...until John" and "since that time" show that the turning point of redemptive history has taken place.

4. The whole ministry of Jesus, in words and works, represents the arrival of the kingdom of God. His ministry of exorcism demonstrates that the kingdom is present (Luke 11:20). His ministry of healing reveals the same (Luke 4:18–20). He announces that the kingdom is present (Mark 1:15). As he moves around Galilee, speaking words and doing works, the kingdom comes.

5. The cross is explained as the Day of Judgement occurring in advance of the final Day of Judgment (John 12:30–33). As he dies, the "end" occurs (John 19:30).[36] The sin of humanity is taken up into him as he is lifted up on the cross.

6. The resurrection is supremely the revelation of the reality of the future age, because Jesus' risen body is the seed and prototype of the resurrection of all the dead in the coming age (1 Corinthians 15:20–22, 42–56; Philippians 3:20–21).

7. The day of Pentecost is described by Peter as a phenomenon of the "last days" and the Day of the Lord (Acts 2:17–21).

---

[35]Or "everyone is strongly urged to enter it", NRSV footnote. N. T. Wright, KNT, translates "From now on, God's kingdom is announced, and everyone is trying to attack it."
[36]The Greek *tetelestai* means "the end", taken from the word *telos*, end.

We can represent the series of kingdom arrivals by this diagram. M&M stands for Jesus' message and ministry.

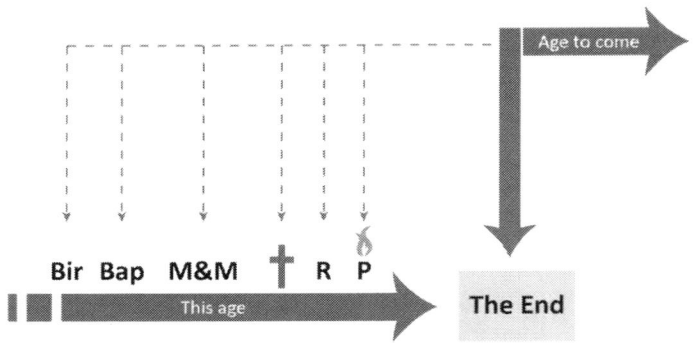

It is of the very nature of the kingdom to break in through a series of interventions of the powers of the coming age (Hebrews 6:4). If we ask, is there "subsequence" here, the answer is yes, there are a whole series of moments, each subsequent to the other.

If we think of how we, as humans and Christians relate to the Holy Spirit, we can also think of a whole series of works of the Spirit.

DIVERSE WORKS OF THE HOLY SPIRIT

A few texts are cited for each point, but in a thorough biblical theology of the Spirit considerably more biblical support could be found for each one.

1. We, and all creatures, relate to the Holy Spirit by virtue of creation (Genesis 1:2; Psalm 33:6; Psalm 104:29, 30).

2. We, and all humans, relate to the Holy Spirit by virtue of human life, making us divine image bearers (Genesis 2:7; Job 34:14–15; Ecclesiastes 12:7).

3. The Holy Spirit relates to unregenerate humanity through conviction of sin (John 16:8,11).

4. The Holy Spirit relates to Christians in terms of regeneration (1 Corinthians 12:13; John 3:3,6).

5. The Holy Spirit relates to Christians in terms of transformation (2 Corinthians 3:18).

6. The Holy Spirit relates to the regenerate person in terms of power for service (Acts 1:8).

7. The Holy Spirit will relate to regenerate humanity in terms of glorification (Ephesians 1:14; 1 Corinthians 15:51–54).

Again, everything could be viewed as "subsequent." However, it would be better to describe each of these as *distinct* aspects of the many-faceted work of the Holy Spirit.[37] To say one work is often subsequent to another work is not at all problematic, just as the series of kingdom interventions is not problematic. Those who want to conflate everything into one work of the Spirit are engaging in reductionism, just as those who select one high point in the life and ministry of Jesus as *the* pivot of the ages are into reductionism (in Protestant theology, often the cross).[38]

The Spirit comes, like the kingdom comes!

We can go further and link the stages of the kingdom's coming to the various distinct works of the Holy Spirit. The ministry of the Spirit is to take what is "of" Jesus and communicate or impart that to us (John 15:26; 16:15). The three high points of the ministry of Jesus each communicate something to us by the Spirit.

1. The death of Jesus brings us forgiveness. We are justified by faith in the blood of Jesus, through the Spirit (Romans 3:21–26; 1 Corinthians 6:11).[39]

2. We are born again through the resurrection of Jesus (1 Peter 1:3).[40] It was the risen Jesus who breathed the new creation into the

---

[37]Notice in the symbolic language of Revelation, the "seven spirits of God" that are identical to the seven lamps (Revelation 1:4; 3:1; 4:5; 5:6) which are effectively, the omnipresence of the lamb.

[38]On reductionism, Morphew, *The Kingdom Reformation*, 402-472.

[39]"You were sanctified, you were justified in the name of the Lord Jesus Christ and by the Spirit of our God."

[40]"In his great mercy he has given us new birth into a living hope through the resurrection of Jesus Christ from the dead."

disciples by the Spirit (John 20:22).[41] Through his resurrection he brought us immortality (2 Timothy 9:1–10).[42]

3. Pentecost pours upon the church the power to execute his Lordship. The climax of Peter's sermon on the day of Pentecost was his declaration: "Therefore let all Israel be assured of this: God has made this Jesus, whom you crucified, both Lord and Messiah" (Acts 2:36). While Jesus will exert his Lordship finally at the end, when every knee will bow (Philippians 2:10–11), as ascended Lord, he "already" rules now.

   Peter makes the connection between the ascension and the nature of Pentecost quite clear. "Exalted to the right hand of God, he has received from the Father the promised Holy Spirit and has poured out what you now see and hear" (Acts 2:33). What comes upon us in Pentecost is the executive power to bring the rule of Christ into this world, so that his will is done on earth as it is in heaven. The prophetic gift of the Spirit enables us to reverse the reality of a broken and fallen world, as we drive out demons, heal the sick, set the captives free and turn the world upside down.[43]

The multifaceted nature of the redeeming work of Christ is enacted in us through diverse works of the Holy Spirit. All is by grace, through faith.

This now sets the stage for us to ask, what exactly is Pentecost? What do we receive when we experience Pentecost?

---

[41]"And with that he breathed on them and said, 'Receive the Holy Spirit.'"

[42]"This grace was given us in Christ Jesus before the beginning of time, but it has now been revealed through the appearing of our Savior, Christ Jesus, who has destroyed death and has brought life and immortality to light through the gospel."

[43]"These people who have been turning the world upside down have come here also... They are all acting contrary to the decrees of the emperor, saying that there is another king named Jesus" (NRSV).

WHAT IS PENTECOST?

Many scholars who have studied Luke-Acts have noticed that Luke draws on and assumes the Old Testament view of the Holy Spirit, particularly as prophetic anointing. Through his terminology and allusions, he intentionally recalls the Old Testament background.[44] Then, within the Old Testament, he draws specifically on the "sons of the prophets" associated with the ministries of Elijah and Elisha.

In the gospel the ministry of Jesus is placed in parallel with the ministry of Elijah and Elisha.

Jesus and Elijah/Elisha

Here are the characteristics of their ministry.

1. Multiplication of food/oil (1 Kings 17:16; 2 Kings 4.1–7, 42–44).

2. Healing of leprosy (2 Kings 5:1–18).

3. Raising to life of a dead child (1 Kings 17:17–24; 2 Kings 4:18–37).

4. Exercise of prophetic gifts of knowledge (2 Kings 5:19–27; 6:12, 32).

5. Power flowing out involuntarily (2 Kings 13:21).

6. Being transported by the Spirit (1 Kings 18:12).

7. The taking up to heaven at the moment of succession and anointing of the Spirit (2 Kings 2:1–14).

Here are the parallels between Elijah/Elisha and Jesus.

---

[44]This point is strongly defended by Robert P. Menzies, *Empowered for Witness, The Spirit in Luke-Acts*, London: T & T Clark, 2004.

Jesus Compared to Elijah/Elisha (Luke 4:25–27)			
Prophetic power	Jesus	Elijah	Elisha
Heals leprosy	Luke 2:12–13		2 Kings 5:14
Multiplies food	Luke 9:16–17	1 Kings 17:16	2 Kings 4:3–7, 42–44
Raises the dead	Luke 8:55	1 Kings 17:22	2 Kings 4:35
Gifts of knowledge	Luke 9:45; Mark 9:33		2 Kings 5:19–27; 6:12, 32
Power flowing out	Luke 6:19; 8:46		2 Kings 13:21
Bodily transportation	Mark 6:48; John 6:19; Matthew 14:25–26	1 Kings 18:12	
Sight of departure	Luke 1:9; Acts 1:9		2 Kings 2:1–14

Pentecost as succession narrative

Given this parallel, we can confidently infer that Luke saw Pentecost as a succession narrative. Just as Elisha "saw" Elijah ascend into heaven, and therefore received a "double portion" of his spirit (2 Kings 2:9), so that the company of the prophets could say, "The spirit of Elijah rests on Elisha" (2 Kings 2:15), the apostles appointed by Jesus saw him being lifted up and taken out of their sight (Acts 1:9). As a result, the messianic anointing that was on Jesus during his ministry was poured out on them at Pentecost.

Another parallel is the succession from Moses to Joshua (Deuteronomy 34:9). Keener explains,

> Although both may form part of the background, however, the transfer of the Spirit from Elijah to Elisha is most relevant, for it is part of the OT's only explicit ascension scene (to which the passing on is explicitly connected; 2 Kgs 2:10,13; cf Sir 48:9,12). Plainly, in view of both these earlier biblical models, Jesus is passing on his prophetic ministry and empowerment to his disciples.[45]

END TIMES PROPHETIC RESTORATION

Peter explains Pentecost by quoting Joel. There can be no doubt therefore

---

[45]Keener, *Acts, Volume 1,* 713.

about the essential nature of Pentecost. A gift that came on certain special servants of God in the Old Testament is now poured out upon "all flesh", namely that they "shall prophesy" (Acts 2:17–18). It is interesting that Luke edits the text of Joel to emphasize certain points. He changes "after these things" (Joel 3:1) to "in the last days"[46] (Acts 2:17). After the naming of male and female slaves he adds the words "and they shall prophesy" (Acts 2:18). Together they show that Luke is referencing the widely held Jewish expectation that in the end times the spirit of prophesy, which had long departed from Israel, would return (1 Maccabees 9:27; 4:45–46; 14:41; 2 Baruch 85:3; Sirach 36:14–16).[47]

> It is impossible to overestimate the importance of earliest Christian prophecy, as the most important phenomenon of the *charismata* given by the Spirit, for the extension of the new Jewish-eschatological movement.[48]

> Luke connects the Spirit especially with prophecy and prophetic types of activity; Jesus appears as a Spirit-anointed (Luke 4:18; Acts 10:38) prophet (Luke 4:24; 13:33; 24:19), and now the church is empowered prophetically as well (Acts 2:17–18). In view of the parallels with Elijah and Elisha in 1:8–11 (also emphasized in the programmatic text for the Gospel, Luke 4:25–27), this would include the sorts of signs associated with those prophets. This fits the ministry of apostles (Acts 2:43; 5:12; 14:3, 15; 15:12) and others in Acts (6:8; 8:6,13).[49]

Prophecy therefore functions as an umbrella term for all the phenomena that fall under it: tongues, healing, revelatory gifts, dreams and visions. In a sense all the charismatic gifts are manifestations of the single Old Testament anointing on the company of the prophets. The church is now the company of the prophets. Because of that identity, it functions in a diversity of prophetic gifts.

---

[46]This gives it a more overtly eschatological meaning.
[47]Keener provides an excursus on these expectations in *Acts, Volume 1*, 886–909.
[48]Ibid., 910, citing Aune.
[49]Ibid., 910.

COMMISSIONING AND EMPOWERING

In the Old Testament background that Luke so clearly alludes to, there are important stories that show the relationship between commissioning and empowering.

In the Old Testament the work of the Spirit was predominantly a work of empowering and anointing for some special task or ability. It is seldom linked with salvation. Further, key figures had an encounter with a theophany (manifestation of God, often called "the angel of the Lord")[50] which functioned as a call, or commission, followed by the anointing of the Spirit coming on them to fulfil that commission.

1. The burning bush experience was a theophany in which *Moses* was commissioned to go and liberate his people from Egypt (Exodus 3:1–4:23). There is repeated use of command language to "go" (3:10,16; 4:12).[51] There is no reference to the anointing of the Spirit on Moses. Then in numbers Numbers 11:14,17 we learn that it is through the Spirit that is on Moses that he is able to carry the people towards their destiny, an anointing now to be placed on the elders to perform this calling alongside Moses.

2. *The Elders* had their own experience of theophany on Mount Sinai (Exodus 24:9–11). This was in the context of the setting up of the covenant (24:1–8) where the people took an oath to obey Yahweh. Then when they are én route to the land of promise, the Lord

---

[50]Here is how J. A. Motyer describes theophany.

It is certainly not inappropriate to note how often the angel is both identified with the Lord (e.g. Genesis 22:11,13) and distinguished from Him (e.g. Genesis 22:15,16). E. Jacob, ...speaks of Him as 'the double of Yahweh' and yet the relationship is not one of simple identity, ...for Exodus 33:1–3 says that the angel (in whom, none the less, is the 'name', the full nature of Yahweh, Exodus 23:31), will go with Israel lest, were Yahweh Himself to go, He would consume them for their provocation. The paradox of this divine angel was not solved until the revelation of Him, Who is both distinct from God and yet identical, Who, without diluting the divine holiness yet kept company with sinners and Who, without denying God's wrath, is yet the supreme outreaching of God's mercy, Jesus Christ, our Lord (*New Bible Commentary,* article on "Old Testament Theology," 29.)

[51]From a literary point of view, this fits into the Old Testament prophetic call narrative form.

poured out the anointing of the Spirit on them to enable them to fulfil what they had promised (Numbers 11:16–25).

3. *Joshua* met the angel of the Lord, the commander of the Lord's army (Joshua 5:13; 6:7). This was similarly an experience of theophany, since Joshua fell on his face to worship him and he spoke as Yahweh (6:2). The entire incident is one of military commission. Then in other texts we learn that Joshua received the anointing of the Spirit through his close association with Moses, rather like the Elijah/Elisha relationship (Numbers 27:18–23). He received the "spirit of wisdom" to fulfil his task through Moses laying hands on him (Deuteronomy 34:9).

4. *Gideon* similarly meets the angel of the Lord (Judges 6:11–24) who is identical to the Lord himself (6:14) and receives worship (6:21). The entire narrative has to do with commissioning for battle (6:14, 16,25). Then as the day of battle arrived "the Spirit of Yahweh took possession of Gideon," empowered him for the task (Judges 6:34). The intervening events show the time gap between the two (Judges 6:33).

5. *Samson's* parents experienced the angel of the Lord/theophany (Judges 13:2,20). The entire narrative is one of commissioning for their son (Judges 13:2–24). Then as Samson is born and grows to maturity "the Spirit of Yahweh began to stir him" (Judges 13:24–25). Then at critical moments the Spirit of the Lord "came mightily on him" (14:6,19; 15:14–15) giving him supernatural strength to perform as a mighty warrior.

6. *Saul* was commissioned to lead Israel when Samuel anointed him with oil (1 Samuel 10:1–2). Then as Saul went from Samuel and entered the company of the prophets the Spirit of the Lord fell on him, making him one of the sons of the prophets (1 Samuel 10:9–13).

The point of these narratives is not to demarcate one phenomenon from the other. Yet it is quite clear that commissioning is the role played by the angel of the Lord, while empowering to fulfil that commissioned task is given by the Spirit of the Lord. Some of the stories show "subsequence" more obviously than others, but the real point is the *distinct* work of the Spirit to empower someone previously commissioned.

31

In the story of Jesus and his disciples, the resurrection encounters are an experience of theophany and commissioning. In Matthew, the mountain top experience (Matthew 28:16) recalls the mountain scene of Moses at Sinai. The commission is given in that context (Matthew 28:18–20). The end of Luke and the beginning of Acts function in the same way. The commission that "repentance and forgiveness of sins is to be proclaimed in his name to all nations" (Luke 24:47), and that they will be his witnesses "to the end of the earth" (Acts 1:8), is given in the context of the cloud of glory taking Jesus up to heaven. Then, on the Day of Pentecost, the prophetic anointing on Jesus is transferred to them, empowering them to fulfil the commission.

Therefore, the term "subsequence" is not ideal. The point is not about the exact timing of the experience, but about its purpose and essential nature. It is better to speak of the *distinctive* nature of the Pentecostal experience.

What is obvious is that Pentecost was not the moment when the disciples were saved or brought into the kingdom of God. They had already been born again and commissioned through the risen Christ (John 20:22). *Pentecost is essentially a prophetic anointing event.* Then, anointed by the Spirit, they evangelized their first three thousand converts (Acts 2:37–42). The anointing "worked", right away. From then on, they carried the anointing that was on Jesus and continued to do what he "began to do and teach" (Acts 1:1).

CHRISTIAN EXPERIENCE

We are now ready to address the question of Christian experience and what you might seek for and expect.

Before we even discuss the experiences of the early church in Acts, we need to think about the relationship between Scripture and experience. All should agree that Scripture has authority over experience. We don't want to develop an experienced based theology, but a biblical theology. However, there is a cyclical relationship between what we see in Scripture (our hermeneutic) and our experience. If our experience is nowhere near the experience of those who were biblical witnesses, then we will be less likely to be able to "get inside" what they were thinking.[52]

The fact is that those who have the privilege of having lived through the kind of revival phenomena that are described in Acts are likely to have a better reading of Acts. This links in with the wisdom of Wesley's Quadrilateral. Wesley taught that we should develop doctrine from four sources: Scripture, tradition, reason, and Christian experience. The history of Christian testimony about the empowering of the Spirit (tradition) and our experience of the empowering of the Spirit is therefore not without its relevance.

The story of Luke-Acts does provide evidence of "subsequence". Here are the cases of possible subsequence.

1. Jesus was born of the Spirit and later anointed by the Spirit (Luke 1:31; 3:21).

2. The disciples were given new creation life by the risen Christ and later empowered by the Spirit at Pentecost (John 20:22; Acts 2).[53]

---

[52]This is covered in Derek Morphew, *Interpretation*, 69–80. Keener discusses this relationship in depth in *Spirit Hermeneutics, Reading Scripture in the Light of Pentecost,* Grand Rapids: Eerdmans, 2016.

[53]Admittedly, this combines a Johannine text with Luke-Acts.

3. The Samaritans were brought to saving faith through the ministry of Philip and later "received the Holy Spirit" through the laying on of hands by Peter and John (Acts 8:12, 14–17).

4. Paul was dramatically converted on the Damascus road (Acts 9:1–9) and later filled with the Spirit when Ananias laid hands on him (Acts 9:10–19).

5. This is a doubtful one, but some say that the household of Cornelius was already in relationship with God, and then baptised in the Spirit when Peter preached to them.

6. The Ephesians were already "disciples", but the Holy Spirit "came on" them when Paul laid his hands on them (Acts 19:1–7).

There are many books written about these cases and many detailed arguments are marshalled by the opposing camps. James Dunn is regarded as the champion of the evangelical camp. He argues that none of these cases prove subsequence.[54] Various Pentecostal scholars argue that they all do.[55] Max Turner and some who have followed him are viewed as representing a kind of mediating position.[56] There are strengths and weaknesses on both sides.

1. The view that the household of Cornelius was already converted is difficult to defend. Here we probably have one clear case of a *simultaneous* experience.

2. The view that the Samaritans were not really converted is very difficult to defend. Here we probably have a clear case of *subsequence*.

3. One of the main weaknesses of the hard evangelical position is that its proponents tend to make every case into an exception, but for

---

[54]James Dunn, *Baptism in the Holy Spirit: A Re-examination of the New Testament on the Gift of the Spirit*, Westminster: John Knox Press, 1977.

[55]For respected Pentecostal and charismatic scholarly works see Howard M. Ervin, *Conversion-Initiation and the Baptism of the Holy Spirit*, Peabody: Hendrickson Publishers, 1984; Robert P. Menzies, *Empowered for Witness: The Spirit in Luke-Acts*, Sheffield: Sheffield Academic Press, 1994; Roger Stronstad, *The Charismatic Theology of St. Luke: Trajectories from the Old Testament to Luke-Acts*; Frank D Macchia, *Baptized in the Spirit: A Global Pentecostal Theology*, Grand Rapids: Zondervan, 2006.

[56]Max Turner, *Power from on High: The Spirit in Israel's Restoration and Witness in Luke-Acts*, Sheffield: Sheffield Academic Press, 1996.

the household of Cornelius. Jesus cannot be our model, because he is unique. The disciples cannot be our model, because they spanned the unique turning point of the ages. The Samaritans are unique because they were a special people group, so the Spirit had to be given by the formal apostolic leadership. Attempts are made to argue that Paul was not really converted before being filled with the Spirit. The Ephesians are unique because they only knew the baptism of John. But when viewed as a whole, this argument looks too much like a refusal to take Luke-Acts seriously because of a Pauline mindset.

4. While there is no clear pattern in the various conversion and initiation stories in Acts, and while not every element is described every time, there does seem to be a broad pattern that people came to faith, then were baptised, and then had hands laid on them for the empowering of the Holy Spirit. At least this is how the post-apostolic church viewed things, because this became the basis of the Catholic and Anglican high church view of confirmation.[57]

But does this mean we must adopt a *doctrine of subsequence*? To agree with Wimber, no it does not. As we have noted, the point is not really subsequence, but the *distinctive* prophetic empowering nature of Pentecost.

If we allow our experience to be a factor, and if one asks around in our churches today, one will find at least five kinds of experience.

1. There are clear "subsequence" people. They can tell you the day and details of their conversion, and they can tell you the day and details of their later empowering of the Holy Spirit (or their

---

[57]J. N. D. Kelly, in *Early Christian Doctrines*, London: Adam & Charles Black, 1968, 433–436, traces the ancient rite of initiation which came to be known as confirmation. According to Kelly, the distinction between the two works of the Spirit (regeneration and anointing) in the two sacraments (baptism and *chrism*) can be traced through Irenaeus (195), Hippolytus (208), Tertullian (209), Cyprian (209), Cyril of Jerusalem (433), Innocent 1 (434), Augustine and Ambrose (435). Bishop Frederick Chase, in *Confirmation and the Apostolic Age* (London: MacMillan and Co, 1909) uses all the texts the Pentecostals use for the baptism in the Spirit to describe the Anglican doctrine of confirmation. The history of this tradition is also examined by Kilian McDonnell and George T. Montague in *Christian Initiation and Baptism in the Holy Spirit: Evidence from the First Eight Centuries,* Collegeville: The Liturgical Press, 1991.

baptism in the Spirit, if they prefer to use Luke's language, which as we have seen, is quite legitimate).

2. There are clear "simultaneous" people. They will describe one experience of coming to faith and an immediate entry into the charismatic dimension of the Spirit (like Cornelius and company).

3. There are "subsequence" plus many fillings people, rather like the disciples were given resurrection life by the risen Christ, filled with the Spirit at Pentecost and again filled with the Spirit in Acts 4.23–31. They will describe a conversion experience, a later entry into the charismatic dimension, and then a series of similar or growing experiences thereafter.[58]

4. There are "simultaneous" plus many fillings people. They will tell of their conversion and then a series of charismatic encounters, none of which to them, was *the* subsequent experience.

5. There are perhaps millions of faithful, committed Christians, who never have any sort of charismatic experience and never function in any clearly charismatic gift. Many of them show more maturity than many charismatically endowed Christians. This is too large a subject to delve into here. One could debate why this may be the case. However, it is important to leave the tension of the New Testament intact and not attempt to resolve it with neat answers. It is also important to not create an "in/out" division.

All these can be justified by the story that Luke, and the wider New Testament tells. None of them should be elevated or deprecated in relation to the others.

It is interesting to see how Wimber adopts this flexible approach.

Baptism is a flexible metaphor not a technical term. Luke seems to regard it as synonymous with fullness (Acts 2:4, cf. 11–16). Therefore, so long as we recognize conversion as truly a baptism in the Spirit, there is no reason why we cannot use baptism to refer to subsequent filling of the Spirit as well. This later experience, or experiences, should not be tied in with the tight second blessing schema, but should be seen as an actualization of what we have already

---

[58]I would fit into this group.

received in the initial charismatic experience, which is conversion.[59]

Notice how Wimber keeps all the options open. Conversion is a baptism in the Spirit. A later "experience" (singular) can be a baptism in the Spirit, or later "experiences" (plural). Then too, one can use the language of "actualizing" a prior reception of the Spirit. He actually endorses three views here.

But, here is the really important point.

Any teaching that says, you have been born again, now you have "got it all", and you must not expect more, or seek a further empowering of the Holy Spirit, is not biblical.

Most of these teachers confuse our position in Christ, which is fully accomplished and all of grace (Colossians 2:9–10), with the actualization of the work of Christ by the Spirit. Jesus commanded us to go beyond knowing him as saviour and Lord. He knew that we could not fulfil his commission without being the recipients of his prophetic anointing. There is a difference between salvation and anointing for service.

HOW DO YOU KNOW?

This then leads to another question. How do you know if you have yet to receive the Pentecostal anointing? Before you read further, you should be assured that only you can really answer that question. On this subject, do not let any pressure be placed on you to conform to a doctrinal position

---

[59]Wimber in Nerheim, 58. This nuanced flexibility might have been lost in some subsequent Vineyard articulations. This statement by Rich Nathan and Ken Wilson, in *Empowered Evangelicals, Bringing Together the Best of the Evangelical and Charismatic Worlds,* Ann Arbor: Vine Books, 1995, 212, removes the "necessary" idea of subsequence and evidence, point well taken, but does not include that subsequence *can be* included as well. Referring to the reality which Pentecostals and charismatics bear witness to, they write:

> That reality is simply this: there's more. Not a "Second Blessing," a baptism in the Spirit necessarily distinct from the new birth, necessarily signified by speaking in tongues; but a lifetime of subsequent and ongoing fillings of the Spirit.

It does not seem to be clear here that *some may* experience a specific subsequent experience, not necessary, but possible, and if one follows Luke-Acts and church history, quite frequent. One could deduce that *only* "a lifetime of ongoing fillings" is to be expected, as the outworking of "multidimensional approach to conversion" based on the views of Thomas Oden.

imposed on you by someone else. As you have just read, a balanced view of the biblical teaching includes a full range of Christian experience. Seek God and ask him to show you the answer.

But here are some helpful clues. While all the characteristics that follow often apply, they do not all occur every time a person is empowered by the Spirit. Some may occur at one point, and others during later experiences of being filled with the Spirit.

1. This is a distinctive work of the Holy Spirit that is more outwardly *manifest* than deeply inward. The true sign of conversion and regeneration is the inner witness the Holy Spirit gives us that we are sons and daughters of God (Galatians 4:6; Romans 8:15). In John's language, we know that we know him (1 John 3:24). In fact, being clear about that is the foundation upon which we should seek all empowering or charismatic experiences. What makes Pentecost distinct is that it is the outpouring that "you see and hear" (Acts 2:33). It comes with certain observable phenomena.

2. The one descriptive term used in Scripture is *to prophesy* (Acts 1:17–18). Speaking in tongues falls under the category of the prophetic. Pentecostals teach that tongues is *the* indispensable sign of Pentecost. But this cannot be defended from Scripture[60] or experience. There are too many stories of people who have clearly been overwhelmed and empowered by the Spirit and not spoken in tongues at the time. Nevertheless, it is the most common phenomenon described in Acts and a common phenomenon in Christian experience today. If you speak in tongues, then you prophesy, and you enter into the prophetic.

3. If we examine how the word "prophecy" is used in the passages that describe this work of the Spirit, we will find that it includes a form of *ecstatic praise*. Samuel describes the empowering that would come on Saul in these words:

> you will meet a procession of prophets coming down from the high place with lyres, timbrels, pipes and harps being played before them, and they will be prophesying (1

---

[60]It cannot be defended from Scripture because there is no text that says this must be the sign. One can only argue from the predominance of cases in Acts.

Samuel 10:5).

As promised, "a procession of prophets met him; the Spirit of God came powerfully upon him, and he joined in their prophesying" (verse 9). Saul had a similar prophetic experience when he was looking for David,

> The Spirit of God came even on him, and he walked along prophesying until he came to Naioth. He stripped off his garments, and he too prophesied in Samuel's presence. He lay naked all that day and all that night. This is why people say, "Is Saul also among the prophets?" (1 Samuel 19:23–24).

Similarly, when Elisha was asked to prophesy by Jehoshaphat king of Judah, he called for a harpist, so that he could enter into worship. "While the harpist was playing, the hand of the Lord came on Elisha" and then he spoke the prophetic word (2 Kings 3:15).

Clearly the form of prophetic speech that is initiated, in the moment, by worship was not the kind of prophetic speech reflected in the great writing prophets. The earliest reference to this kind of prophetic behaviour is when the Spirit came on the seventy elders and the two in the camp of Israel (Number 11:25–26). The Hebrew word is a form of verb taken from the noun, "prophet", which means literally "to act the prophet."[61] It was a speaking forth, almost involuntarily, under the overwhelming power of the Holy Spirit. The musicians in David's day were said to "prophesy with lyres, harps, and cymbals" (2 Chronicles 25:1–2), they "prophesied with the lyre in thanksgiving and praise to the Lord" (1 Chronicles 25:3).

On the day of Pentecost, they were similarly overcome (appearing to be drunk) and spoke forth the "wonders of God" (Acts 2:14). Peter knew that the Gentiles had been filled with the Spirit "For they heard them speaking in tongues and praising God" (Acts 10:46). This suggests that speaking in tongues is a form of prophetic speech or praising God. Similarly, the Ephesians "spoke in tongues and prophesied" (Acts 19:6). The phenomenon can be

---

[61]Timothy R. Ashley, *The Book of Number, The New International Commentary,* Grand Rapids: Eerdmans, 1993, 213–214.

ecstatic speech not in the speaker's language, or a form of ecstatic praise in the speaker's language.

4. It is a "coming on" or "falling" of the Spirit that often *overwhelms* the person in a way that affects the human body, mind and emotions (Acts 2:15). Many biblical texts and many experiences of Christians through the centuries describe something that is manifest in the body. People may tremble or shake, fall, experience heat or waves of energy,[62] or appear to stand motionless.[63] Such bodily sensations are often accompanied by a sense of delight in God and God's delight in us, so the mind and emotions are also engaged. Also common is a sense of ecstatic joy, which explains the common phenomenon of pouring out praise, or declaring how great God is. Sometimes this leads to being overwhelmed with laughter.

5. The empowering of the Spirit often comes through *the laying on of hands.* There is such a thing as impartation. This was the case with the Samaritans (Acts 8:17), Paul (9:17) and the Ephesians (19:6) and Moses/Joshua in the Old Testament. Closely associated with laying on of hands is the phenomenon of a space or zone of power, so that as people approach it, they come under the power of the Spirit. This is described in the phenomena that accompany many revivals.

In the larger theology of the kingdom of God we learn that revivals are repeat Pentecost's. Therefore, phenomena that frequently take place in revivals are Pentecostal phenomena. They are the *church history* of being filled and empowered with the Holy Spirit.

We should recall what was said earlier about the diversity of Christian experience. These "manifest" signs of the prophetic empowering of the Spirit in the Old Testament and in Luke-Acts are not the whole story. Many Christians never have such a "manifest" prophetic charismatic

---

[62]Elijah was able to outrun Ahab's chariot because "the hand of the Lord" was on him (1 Kings 18:46).

[63]When Solomon dedicated the temple, the priests "could not stand to minister because of the cloud; for the glory of the Lord filled the house of God" (2 Chronicles 5:17 NRSV). Saul "lay naked all day and all night", clearly overcome (2 Samuel 19:23–24). The NRSV translates the text about the various messengers that Saul sent to find David as, "they fell into a prophetic frenzy" (1 Samuel 18:19–24).

experience, yet faithfully serve God and are used by him in all sorts of ways. We should neither water down Luke's mix of criteria, nor make that the only teaching about the Spirit in the New Testament.

POWER FOR MINISTRY

While these are the biblical and historical phenomena, we must be very careful not to make them our focus. They happen *to come along with* the empowering of the Spirit. If this is what we seek, then we might seek in vain. What is much more important is the test or result, the criterion of this empowering. That, Jesus declares, is *power to witness,* or as we have learned from Luke's theology, receiving prophetic empowering. Other biblical texts describe boldness to act for God. When we ask for the Holy Spirit to come on us our one and only focus must be power for service; boldness to fulfil the commission.

The moment Peter was filled with the Spirit he "raised his voice and addressed the crowd" (Acts 2:14), a sudden change from the broken figure of the trial narrative. He had boldness to say to a crippled man, "In the name of Jesus Christ of Nazareth, walk" (Acts 3:6). "Filled with the Spirit" he spoke fearlessly to the rulers and elders of the people (4:8), who "saw the courage of Peter and John" (4:13). When told not to speak further in the name of Jesus, he replied "We must obey God rather than human beings!" (5:29). He had courage to say to Aeneas, "Jesus Christ heals you. Get up and roll up your mat" (9:34), and to a dead disciple, "Tabitha, get up" (9:40).

Such boldness is the New Testament parallel to the way Old Testament judges and prophets went out to battle when the Holy Spirit came on them.

When the Spirit of the Lord came on Othniel, he "became Israel's leader and went to war" (Judges 3:10). When the Spirit of the Lord came on Gideon he blew the trumpet and summoned Israel to war (Judges 6:34–35). The same occurred when the Spirit of God came on Jephthah (Judges 11:29). When "the Spirit of the Lord came on Jahaziel son of Zechariah" he told Jehoshaphat king of Judah, "Do not be afraid or discouraged because of this vast army. For the battle is not yours, but God's" (2 Chronicles 20:14–15). After he was anointed by Samuel "the Spirit of the Lord came powerfully upon David" (1 Samuel 16:13). He became mighty in battle[64] and the Lord gave him victory wherever he went (2 Samuel 8:6,14).

Our battle is not against human foes but the powers of darkness that hold humanity prisoner (Luke 11:17–22; Ephesians 6:12). Our commission is to set the captives free and bind up the broken hearted (Luke 4:18–19).

The Pentecostal empowering of the Spirit is often the gateway into the charismatic gifts, which fill out the details of the prophetic. Gifts of revelation, healing and deliverance empower the mission of the gospel.

One of the disadvantages of having a fixed doctrine of "subsequence" is that it might lead to the idea that only one experience of being filled is necessary. But the story of Acts points to "many fillings." As is often said, we tend to "leak."

This type of filling is not to be equated with our regular devotional walk with God. Luke emphasises the communal nature of these events.[65] Yes, we can be filled with the Spirit, in a genuinely Pentecostal manner, when we are alone with God. There are many testimonies of people being filled in this way.[66] But the pattern in Acts is a church event. The leaders of the church, aware of the command of Jesus and of our desperate need for God's power, lead their people into a specific time of prayer, and then when all are gathered in unity of purpose, they lay hands on them for impartation.

Prayer for the filling of the Spirit is the responsibility of those who disciple new believers. In the early church it usually followed baptism. In the later church, the sequence was catechism, baptism, and confirmation/anointing. If we do not teach that Pentecostal empowering is available, and to be expected, and if we do not facilitate times of focused prayer for its reception, then we should not be surprised if the church is not endued with charismatic gifts. We need to create the expectation amongst our people by clearly teaching about Pentecost, and we need to create opportunities for them to receive empowering through impartation and the laying on of hands. A water baptism that is not followed immediately[67] by a time of

---

[64]"And the women sang to one another as they made merry, 'Saul has killed his thousands, and David his ten thousand's'" (1 Samuel 18:7).

[65]The Spirit came on the first Jewish disciples at Pentecost, then the Samaritans, then the Gentiles, each time symbolizing their incorporation into the mission of the kingdom.

[66]That was my experience.

[67]By "immediately" I mean either as they come out of the water, or shortly thereafter, giving

prayer for the empowering of the Spirit is not a fully New Testament baptism.

EXCURSES ON OLD TESTAMENT PHENOMENA OF THE SPIRIT

Many scholars do not know what to do with this element of the Old Testament witness. They seem to have a negative perception of this form of ecstatic speech, and often attempt to contrast this kind of prophetic activity from the later, great prophets. Ashley does not know quite what to conclude from Numbers 11.[68] The article on "Prophet" in the NIDNNT, noting that the verb *naba* is derived from the noun, *nabi*, "which means to show, present, or express oneself, to speak as a prophet", puts it like this:

> In early texts the dominant use is in the hithpael, meaning to behave as a prophet, implying adopting ecstatic behaviour. In later texts the niph'al predominates...This may suggest that in early times prophecy was dominated by ecstatic behaviour which later became suspect. Later still (from Jeremiah onwards) the verb no longer suggested ecstasy and could be used without embarrassment.[69]

A fuller treatment of this subject is found in the work on Old Testament prophecy by E. J. Young.[70] While now dated, his stature as an Old Testament scholar was unparalleled in his day, amongst evangelicals. A few citations might be of interest. One notices that Young must have been far removed from experiences of such phenomena, as he keeps using the term "abnormal behaviour" and is not sure how worship and the prophetic are connected. Also interesting is that he thinks the phenomenon might have been speaking in tongues and was similar to Pentecost. He begins this section on the seventy elders in Numbers 11:24–26, by commenting as follows:

> From the context it is clear that in this case, whatever the exact nature of "prophesying" was, it was not proclaiming the message of a superior. For, in reporting the affair to Moses, the young man

---

them time to change and then having a time of prayer with them.

[68] Ashley, 214.

[69] NIDNNT, Volume 3, 77.

[70] E. J. Young, *My Servants the Prophets,* Grand Rapids: Eerdmans, 1965, 68–75.

employed a participial form (*mithnabb'im*), which implies continuous action. "Eldad and Medad," we may paraphrase, "are now engaged in prophesying in the camp." For some reason these two, although they had been conscripted, remained behind in the camp, and there prophesied. It is very difficult to see how their actions can be equated with preaching.

What then, was the nature of the prophesying? To answer this question we must consider carefully all that the text says. For one thing Moses is here presented in distinction from the others as a man who possesses the Spirit. God withdrew or set apart of His Spirit which rested upon Moses, and set His Spirit upon the seventy elders. This was not for the purpose of rebuking Moses, nor does the action in any sense signify a diminution of the Spirit as possessed by Moses. It was rather, as Dillmann has observed, an impartation of the Spirit in the best sense of the word. In order that the seventy might work with Moses in one spirit and purpose, they were equipped with the same Spirit which had filled him.

When the Spirit thus rested upon them they began to prophesy. The act of prophesying, then, is the direct result of the impartation of the Spirit. According to Heinisch this was a state of ecstatic rapture. Such rapture, however, must have assumed some outward expression, and possibly we are to understand that the seventy spoke in an elevated state of mind, perhaps giving utterance in tongues, as was the case at Pentecost, when the Spirit of God came upon men. The seventy did not add; that is they did not repeat the prophesying further.[71]

He then goes on to discuss the texts about Samuel and Saul.

Surely one cannot conceive of "prophesying" in this context, as an act of preaching. It is difficult to perceive the relationship between the instruments of music and the act of prophesying. It may be that the presence of the musical instruments and the playing upon them brought upon the prophets the ability to prophesy. More likely, however, the actual act of prophesying took some form of singing or ecstatic utterance.[72]

[71]Ibid., 69–70.
[72]Ibid., 70.

Saul would act in such a way, whether through ecstatic utterances, cries, songs or even bodily behaviour, that those who saw him would regard him as a prophet.[73]

Like the other passages which we have been considering, this one also makes it clear that the verb "to prophesy" may be used to characterize strange behaviour. In this instance attention is directed particularly to Saul, who stripped off his garments and fell down naked. Whatever the nature of the state which was thus brought upon Saul, it was an abnormal one, and this condition of abnormality was at times a characteristic of those who were called "prophets" and who "prophesied".[74]

The term *nibbe'im* is also used to describe those who played upon musical instruments in the worship of God… It is difficult to give to the term in this instance its precise significance. Does it indicate that the musicians were overpowered by the Divine Spirit and so under His compulsion played for God's glory and praise? Or, is the thought rather that in "prophesying" with musical instruments, the players were telling forth the praises of God? In all probability the first alternative is correct but it is not clear that the latter should be excluded entirely. At any rate, the term is not employed in a technical sense, and the passage is illuminating in that it permits one to see how widely the concept might be held.[75]

He summarizes at the end by saying,

From a consideration of the denominative verb "to prophesy" we learn that behaviour, which to us seems abnormal, was at times characteristic of the prophets. This was the case particularly in the time of Samuel and in connection with the bands of prophets. It applied also, however, to Jeremiah.[76]

In a later section Young denies the extreme views of some scholars that describe a shaman like state of frenzy, but nevertheless accepts a form of being overcome by the Spirit.

If we employ the word "ecstasy" to describe the prophets, we must

---

[73]Ibid., 71.
[74]Ibid., 73–74.
[75]Ibid., 74–75.
[76]Ibid., 75.

use the word with care… It is without a doubt true that when the Spirit of God thus came upon a man, that man was in an abnormal condition.

There was resting upon him a Divinely imposed compulsion so that he could not but speak forth and sing the wondrous works of God. To this extent we may agree the prophet was in a state of ecstasy.[77]

To the bystander, the strange condition of Saul was like that of the prophets when the Spirit came upon them. For this reason, even though it is not here expressly stated that the prophets fell down naked and lay thus all day and night, it may be assumed that at times this was the case. To the bystander, Saul's condition was reminiscent of the condition which at times came upon the prophets, and for this reason they asked, "Is Saul also among the prophets?"[78]

---

[77]Ibid., 86.
[78]Ibid., 90.

THE THOMAS LYONS THESIS

Thomas Lyons is a member of a Vineyard church in Kentucky, is a regular contributor to the Society of Vineyard Scholars, has taught New Testament Greek at Asbury Seminary and his doctoral dissertation was submitted to Asbury Seminary in February 2020.[79] His mentor was Craig Keener.

Since *Demonstrating the Kingdom* (the above chapter) was published in 2019, Thomas's thesis represents a further development of thought within the post-Wimber tradition. It continues, broadly, within the tradition but offers fresh insights.

There is both continuity and discontinuity with the initiative taken by Wimber, and the way I seek to follow that initiative in *Demonstrating the Kingdom*.

CONTINUITY AND DISCONTINUITY

Continuity

Wimber's view, that Paul and Luke use the term "baptism in the Spirit" differently, and that there is therefore more than one view of the work of the Spirit, is affirmed. This position therefore diverges from traditional conservative evangelical assumptions, where Paul is read into Luke.

Luke's view of the Spirit, as fundamentally prophetic empowering, rather than affecting conversion, is affirmed. In that sense Thomas sides with Pentecostal and charismatic scholarship.

The clearly demarcated notion of subsequence in Pentecostal theology, with tongues as the necessary sign, is repudiated. However, the notion that Spirit reception is not the same as conversion, and is often subsequent, is

---

[79]Thomas Lyons, *Revisting the Riddle in Samaria: A Social-Scientific Investigation of Spirit Reception in Luke-Acts in Historical Perspective*, A Dissertation Presented to the Faculty of Asbury Theological Seminary, Wilmore, KY, February 2020.

affirmed.

In broad terms, Thomas reads the primary cases of Pentecost, the Samaritans, the household of Cornelius, and the Ephesian disciples of John, much as I do.

Discontinuity

The points of discontinuity should not be understood as representing disagreement, but rather as making a fresh contribution, further nuancing the overall position.

Because the term "baptism in the Spirit" is only used three times by Luke, and because of the fraught nature of disagreements around this phrase, Thomas chooses to select "Spirit reception" as his primary term.

While Pentecost (Acts 2), the Samaritans (Acts 8), the Gentiles (Acts 10) and the disciples of John (Acts 19) are regarded as primary cases of Spirit reception, a major argument he makes is that the repeat filling of the Spirit in Acts 4 must be included, making five primary cases. He says this text has been largely ignored by scholars.

The case of Paul being filled with the Holy Spirit is not regarded as a primary case. This enables Thomas to affirm that all the cases of Spirit reception in Acts are corporate or community events.

Probably the most significant contribution of his thesis relates to the nature of Luke-Acts as historical documents. Because Luke is functioning as a historian, his work is more descriptive than deliberately systematic and theological. Luke is not therefore attempting to present an "order of salvation" or affirming a clearly defined order of Christian initiation. The diversity of his descriptions reflects the diversity of his sources. This enables Thomas to lend further weight to Wimber's view, that "there is in Scripture no discernible pattern or formula for how the Spirit falls on us."[80]

Associated with this, and a development of it, is his use of social-scientific tools to draw an analogy between the descriptions of Spirit reception in Acts and similar descriptions in later revivals. He shows that there is the same diversity and flexibility in the phenomena, within an overall continuity or similarly. This is then used to argue backwards into Acts to justify a non-systematic presentation by Luke.

---

[80]Cited in Doug Erickson, *Living the Future*, 153, from John Wimber, *Power Points*, New York: Harper Collins, 1991, 137.

There are some questions that arise, which lend themselves to further dialogue.

He does not emphasise Luke as a theologian, and makes scant reference to redactional readings of Luke,[81] which usually draw conclusions about deliberate emphases or tendencies in Luke-Acts, reflecting Luke's special theological concerns. Where Howard Marshall spoke of Luke, Historian *and* Theologian, Thomas gives more focus to Luke as historian, and gives less focus to Luke as theologian. This is probably the major aspect of his thesis that calls for further dialogue. It raises questions about narrative theology as the basis of theological formulation and the nature of "all Scripture" as "profitable for teaching" (2 Timothy 3:16). We will return to this later.

With this general introduction, we can now explore his work in more detail.

HISTORICAL RESEARCH

Thomas provides some valuable historical research into the history of the interpretation of Acts. He surveys scholars who have contributed to relevant ideas about Spirit reception.[82] The following table lists the scholars he surveys and the dates of their primary publications. Clearly this is a selective list. He interacts with a much wider list of scholars overall.

The History of scholarship on Acts, Thomas Lyons 2020		
Scholar	Language/Country	Date
Herman Gunkel	German	1888
Hans Leisegang	German	1922
Friedrich Büchsel	German	1926
Hans von Baer	German	1926

[81]There is one reference to redactional readings on Luke in the main text. He criticizes Dunn for giving "very little consideration for redactional or narratological issues", Lyons, 9. He has contributed a chapter in a compendium publication where he examines a case of Lukan redaction, "The Rhetoric of Redaction: A Rhetorical Analysis of Redaction in Luke 8:40-56," in *Essays Exploring New Testament Texts*, Wilmore, KY: GlossaHouse, 2019, 37–60. He is clearly fully aware of redactional and narrative readings of Luke-Acts.

[82]"I will survey the main voices that would advance or challenge prevailing positions", Ibid., 3.

James Dunn	English, UK	1970
Roger Stronstad	English, Canada*	1984
Max Turner	English, UK	1980
Howard Ervin	English, USA*	1984
Robert Menzies	English, USA*	1991
Youngmo Cho	English, South Korea*	2005
Aaron Kuecker	English, USA	2011
David McCollough	English, USA*	2017

What is interesting about this list is how the dominating thinkers for the earlier period are German, which is often the case. Then there is the pivotal influence of James Dunn. Then there are various positions adopted in reaction to Dunn. Among them are Pentecostal scholars, demarcated by the Asterisk.*

There are two important contributions by German scholars. Gunkel noticed that there is often a separation between being a believer and receiving the Spirit.[83] This is an intriguing bit of information. Less than twenty years before the Pentecostal revival, featuring the "baptism in the Spirit" as a "subsequent" experience, a German scholar with no such connections was articulating a similar idea. As I have shown in *Breakthrough*, the Pentecostals adopted this from Edward Irving, who taught at the beginning of the 19th Century.[84] There are therefore two reasons for arguing that the Pentecostals had historical precedent, or were not alone in drawing this conclusion from Acts. Further, as shown in a previous chapter, there is a much older precedent for subsequence, namely in the historical Catholic and anglo-Catholic teaching on confirmation. This is by no means a novel idea.

Hans von Baer noticed that "the 'Spirit of Prophecy' was key to understanding the origin and experiences of the Spirit in Luke's materials."[85] This is an insight that has become central to Pentecostal scholarship. It is vigorously presented by Roger Stronstad and Robert Menzies. I noticed that Menzies similarly begins his work by reviewing the history of scholarship. He adds some important details about Gunkel. Gunkel sought to answer the question: "What were the symptoms by which earliest

---

[83]Ibid., 4.
[84]*Breakthrough*, the chapter on "Cessationism." Irving's ministry began in 1830.
[85]Lyons, 7.

Christianity determined that a phenomenon was an activity of the Spirit?"[86] His answer was, "the mysterious and powerful nature of deeds which defied natural explanation" and that tongues was the most characteristic aspect of the gift of the Spirit.[87] Further, Gunkel points out that in the context of contemporary Judaism, these were signs of the in-breaking of the kingdom of God. "Where the Spirit is, there is the kingdom of God."[88]

Menzies, like von Baer, gives considerable attention to expectations within Second Temple Judaism and argues that the primary expectation, found in all the sources, was the restoration of prophecy.[89] He then shows how consistently Luke elevates this theme throughout Luke and Acts.[90] Some have argued that Menzies has pushed this too far, but as Thomas shows, there is now considerable scholarly support for this view.[91]

These readings of Luke are then reversed by James Dunn, who collapses all the cases of Spirit reception into affecting conversion, with the result that the Samaritan experience, with its obvious delay, becomes a riddle. The influence of Dunn on subsequent scholarship becomes evident with Max Turner, whose early Pentecostal church experience and tendency towards a charismatic view of Luke-Acts gradually bent towards Dunn. While his earlier work suggested a mediating position between the Reformed/evangelical view and the Pentecostal/charismatic view, in the end, he followed Dunn.[92]

Thomas's review also shows that he is fully aware of the problem of

---

[86]Menzies, 19, citing Gunkel.

[87]Ibid.

[88]Ibid, citing Gunkel.

[89]Ibid., diaspora literature (49-63), Palestinian literature (63-70), Qumran literature (71-82), Rabbinic literature (83-103).

[90]Ibid., 104-225.

[91]"Against this host of formulaic readings of Spirit reception as conversion-initiation, a large number of voices have proposed that Spirit reception in Luke-Acts generally, including the account found in Acts 8, ought to be read as some type of charismatic empowerment for mission. Included in this grouping of scholars are the likes of Howard Ervin, Roger Stronstad, Robert Menzies, Craig Keener and Youngmo Cho, along with many other Pentecostal and charismatic scholars." Ibid., 34.

[92]Thomas writes, "Where Turner's prior work might be considered 'generally consonant with a classical Pentecostal doctrine of subsequence,' his *Power from on High: The Spirit in Israel's Restoration and Witness in Luke-Acts* (1996) contribution shifts Turner significantly closer to Dunn", Lyons, 14.

Protestant/evangelical writers reading Paul into Luke. He notices how Ervin, Turner and Stronstad criticise Dunn for reading Luke through Pauline lenses.[93]

It is in reviewing the last two scholars in his list that Thomas exposes his primary thesis. There are two key points. First, Luke must be read more as a historian, rather than someone attempting to write a systematic theology. Second, Luke is describing corporate, not individual Spirit reception. The two ideas are interrelated.

On the first point, Thomas notes a valid criticism Dunn makes about McCollough, namely his "lack of awareness or attention to the inherently historical character of Luke-Acts as a two-part work of ancient historiography"[94] and suggests that "the range and diversity of accounts found within the Luke-Acts text is more reflective of historical peculiarity and diversity of witness found in Luke's sources than in any specific systematic theological formulation".[95]

The second point arises from the work of Aaron Kuecker, who elevates the corporate, rather than individual nature of Luke's descriptions of Spirit reception. Thomas agrees with Kuecker's observation that,

> the focus on individual conversion has sought a systematic "order of salvation" with regard to the temporal relationship between repentance, baptism, and Spirit-reception. Yet Luke has written a historical narrative of God's providential creation of a new kind of community, not a systematic pneumatology. Luke's concern is less with a dogmatic "order of salvation" and more with how and why a diverse collection of persons were incorporated into the Spirit-empowered Jesus community.[96]

These remarks then form the basis of his methodological approach, namely, to use social-scientific and interdisciplinary methods for the study of Acts.[97]

---

[93]Ibid., 15.

[94]Ibid., 22. It is interesting to note that McCollough's doctoral dissertation at Durham University seems to be more aligned to Thomas's thesis, as articulated in his self-profile, https://www.dur.ac.uk/theology.religion/staff/profile/

[95]Ibid., 38.

[96]Ibid., 25.

[97]"For such broader historical, sociological, and anthropological concerns, social-scientific interdisciplinary interpretive methods seem to be the best interpretive tools." Ibid., 38.

SPIRIT RECEPTION IN LUKE-ACTS

The four primary cases in Acts usually examined by scholars are,

1. Pentecost (Acts 2)

2. The Samaritans (Acts 8)

3. The household of Cornelius (Acts 10), and

4. The Ephesian disciples of John the Baptist (Acts 19).

However, the filling of the Spirit in Acts 4 (the shaking house) is normally ignored.[98] It is important to add this case, making a total of five.

Since Thomas teaches New Testament Greek to graduate students, he is quite "into" the Greek terminology and grammar. He carefully examines the terms Luke uses in Luke-Acts and how they appear in the five cases in question.[99] The following table describes the terms and where they appear.

Spirit Reception language in Luke-Acts		
Greek terms	**English**	**Texts**
Βαπτιζω/ baptizō	Baptize	Luke 3:16, Acts 1:5, and 11:16
Λαμβανω/lambanō	Receive	Acts 2:38; 8:15, 17, 19; 10:47; 19:2
Πιμπλημι/pimplēmi	Filled	Acts 2:4, but also Luke 1:15, 41, 67 and Acts 9:17; 4:31.
Εκχεω/ekcheō	Pour out	Acts 2:17, 18; 2:33, 10:45
Διδωμι/didōmi	Given	Acts 8:18,19; 11:17
Δωρεά/dōrea,	Gift	Acts 2:38, 8:20, 10:45, 11:17
Χριω/chriō	Anointed	Luke 4:18; Acts 4:27; 10:38
Επιπιπτω/epipiptō	Fell	Acts 8:16, 10:44; 11:15
ἔρχομαι ὁ ἐπί/ erchomai ho epi	Came on	Acts 19.6
ἐνδύω/ endyō	Clothed	Luke 24:49
Επαγγελια/epangelia	The promise	Luke 24:49; Acts 1:4; 2:33, 39

As many have noted, these various terms converge in the five cases,

---

[98]"It is striking how neglected the Spirit reception event of Acts 4:31 has been over the last fifty years with respect to discussions about the nature of Spirit reception." Ibid., 110.

[99]I will not distinguish between verbs and nouns, as he does.

making it impossible to argue that they mean one thing in one Spirit reception but something else in another. Key to Thomas' argument is that Acts 4 does not differ at all from the other accounts. "Luke in no appreciable way differentiates this account linguistically, conceptually, or structurally from the other accounts."[100]

Then each of the five reception accounts are examined. My purpose here is not to repeat all the details of Thomas' treatment, but to select certain key points.

Pentecost

There are four pertinent points made here.

1. Acts 1:4-8, and especially verse 8, is of major significance as the background to Acts 2.

2. Based on this, "Many scholars recognize the essential activity of the Spirit in Luke-Acts as empowering witness for missional proclamation and engagement with the world."[101]

3. Spirit reception "has discernible elements that are perceptible to observers."[102]

4. Luke did not describe the filling of the Spirit promised in Acts 2:38. One cannot argue that it did or did not happen. "Regardless, there is nothing in the character of the future promise of the Spirit by Peter in 2:38 that suggests there cannot be some delay between repentance and baptism and Spirit reception."[103]

The shaking house, Acts 4

After comparing the description with Pentecost, certain key points arise.

Those, like Dunn, who collapse all Spirit reception accounts into conversion/initiation must explain this event as essentially different. However, "The problem with such a reading is that it is not supported lexically or

---

[100]Ibid., 114.
[101]Ibid., 118.
[102]Ibid., 126.
[103]Ibid., 128.

narratively."[104]

It follows that this text is one of the strongest cases for multiple receptions or empowerments by the Spirit. This once again underlines that Luke,

> understand Spirit reception as empowerment of mission, which would include bold proclamation alongside miraculous healings and the working of signs and wonders, the very thing that is requested in the petition portion of the prayer immediately prior (4:29-30) and that which was promised by Jesus before departing (1:8).[105]

The Samaritans, Acts 8

It is commonly argued by Dunn and those who follow him that the Samaritans were not truly converted prior to Peter and John laying hands on them. The problem with this view is that they are described as "receiving the word of God" which Luke uses three time to refer to believing or accepting the gospel (8:14; 11:1; 17:11).

Another popular view, suggested by G. W. H. Lampe, was that the situation in Samaria was unique because it constituted a turning point in the progression of the gospel, and therefore required apostolic involvement. But Thomas finds, "this lacking primarily because Philip in the very next pericope is ministering to the Ethiopian eunuch in the absence of apostles."[106] One need only to reflect on the equally valid "turning point" of the gospel going to a whole new continent! No apostles were needed for that.

The household of Cornelius, Acts 10

Thomas considers the possibility that Cornelius was already converted, which would make Spirit reception again "subsequent." A case can be made for this. Even Calvin argued that Cornelius was accepted by God and knew Christ. However, the actual moment of salvation/conversion is not narrated by Luke. His main point is that the reception of the Spirit bore witness of the fact that they had become believers and should therefore be

---

[104]Ibid., 136.
[105]Ibid., 136.
[106]Ibid., 149.

accepted into the Christian community.

The Ephesian disciples, Acts 19

The status and identity of these "believers" has long been debated. Some argue that they were true believers, others argue that they were not. Interestingly most of those who argue that they were not believers do so on the basis of Pauline texts. But Thomas says,

> The problem with such a reading is that it assumes Dunn's conversion-initiation hypothesis, reads Pauline theology into Luke's material, and ignores instances where there were clearly believers who (even if only for a time) lacked the Holy Spirit (8:16).[107]

While it is possible to nuance the grammar of the Greek text to suggest that there was some sort of ambiguity about them, the term "believed" (Acts 19.2) in "thirty one of the other thirty six occurrences in Acts are clearly in reference to the salvific belief of those who have responded to the gospel".[108]

Conclusions

Having examined the five cases, Thomas then draws his conclusions. Here are some of the significant points.

1. All these accounts are about corporate events. As noted above, one can come to this conclusion by excluding the case of Paul, and also Jesus.

2. "In these accounts, the Spirit is only poured out on those who are believers, that is individuals who have proclaimed their allegiance to Jesus either through water baptism (Acts 2, 4, 8, 19) or by faith in their hearts (Acts 10). For some who receive the Spirit, they have been faithful to Jesus for some period of time (Acts 2, 4, 8), while for others their faith response is fairly recent (Acts 10, 19)."[109]

---

[107]Ibid., 179.
[108]Ibid., 184-5.
[109]Ibid., 191.

3. While there is a relationship between the work of the Spirit and conversion, "Spirit reception does not 'effect' conversion".[110] "Luke portrays those who are 'in' as those 'who received the word of God,' 'who are being saved,' or simply 'who believed.' Salvation as portrayed in Acts is predicated on calling upon the name of the Lord (Acts 2:21; 16:31), on being allegiant to Jesus, not on receiving God's Spirit (in Lukan language). Spirit reception is instead portrayed as empowerment for testifying to Jesus and good news of His Kingdom so that all may be saved (Acts 1:8; 8:12)."[111]

4. Those who receive the Spirit exhibit phenomena such as "tongues/glossolalic vocalizations, prophetic utterances, and bold proclamations."[112] There are likely other phenomena not described by Luke, but which made the event observable to others, things they either saw or heard.

5. "Despite the unique significance of tongues, it is not the most common type of witness phenomena within Luke's accounts. Instead, that honor goes to bold proclamation of the gospel, which is closely associated with every Spirit reception account in Acts, either preceding and prompting the reception event, or following it."[113]

6. The most consistent element in all the accounts is prayer. It either precedes or accompanies the event.

7. Often associated with prayer is a period of waiting for the empowering of the Spirit. "Sometimes this period of time is a mere couple of days (Acts 10), while other times the period of time is numbered in weeks or even months (Acts 2, 8). The longest of these instances is the wait leading up to the first reception at Pentecost, which Jesus himself both set their expectation (Acts 1:8) and commanded them to wait (1:4). This time of waiting is presumably filled with prayer (1:14)."[114]

---

[110]Ibid.
[111]Ibid., 191.
[112]Ibid., 192.
[113]Ibid., 193.
[114]Ibid., 195.

8. Water baptism often precedes Spirit reception, but sometimes not. It is therefore distinguishable from Spirit reception. It does not confer the Spirit. "For Luke, this practice of Christian water baptism contained elements of repentance and declarations of faith/allegiance to Jesus, along with likely involving a preparatory element of ritual washing to prepare for the reception of the Holy Spirit."[115]

Overall, if one condenses all the descriptions, they can be classified into three essential phenomenological categories:

1. Witness (bold proclamation, praising God, prophetic activity, tongues),

2. Power (signs and wonders, healings, exorcisms), and

3. Presence (tangible manifestations).

Having established the nature of Spirit reception in Acts, Thomas then proceeds to describe four revivals.

CHRISTIAN REVIVALS

For various reasons, he decides not to include the Pentecostal revival, or the "Toronto" revival, both of which might be a little too close to those who often weigh in on these matters. Instead he examines the following revivals.

1. The Welsh Revival (1905-06) in the U.K.,

2. The East African Revival (1930s-1950s) in Rwanda, Uganda, and Kenya,

3. the Dayak Revival (1970-1980s) in Malaysia, and

4. The Asbury Revival (1970) in the United States.

These revivals are examined through the lens of the three categories of witness, power and presence. While there is considerable diversity between them, these three categories are to be found in all of them. His account of these revivals makes for exceedingly edifying reading, leaving one

---

[115]Ibid., 196.

astounded at the ways and deeds of God.

The dramatic accounts of God's presence have some diversity, for instance healing (Dayak and Asbury), prophecy (Welsh and Asbury), tongues (East African and Dayak), and dramatic environmental signs (Welsh and Dayak). "For some, the dramatic encounter with the Spirit of God is what initiated their conversion while others report having been believers for years before experiencing the Spirit so dramatically."[116]

Consistent through them all is the emphasis on prayer and waiting on God to act, and repentance. The common experience is that believers are compelled to share their experience. They are empowered to witness. Often the revival brings about community reconciliation. Often the revivals have powerful social impacts. Drawing it all together,

> What can be affirmed from this study is that the phenomenological profile, including associated contextual elements, reported phenomena, praxes, sequence, timing and consequences, of the studied encounters with the Holy Spirit in revival accounts matches the phenomenological profile of similar activity reported by Luke in the Acts data set.[117]

It is when Thomas gets to his final conclusions that we are taken back to the Wimber initiative, namely neither typical evangelical, not classical Pentecostal. He reminds us of Dunn's position, that Spirit reception should be understood as "conversion/initiation" and the Pentecostal position, where speaking in tongues is the norm. But he says, we must remember that Luke is a historian describing the diversity of phenomena.

> I found that the internal range of diverse religious experience within these historic revivals in fact mirrors the range found within the Acts data set. Despite the vast diversity of experiences within each data set, there was also a remarkable amount of continuity across all data sets, further reinforcing the legitimacy of the comparison.[118]

In summary, there is diversity but also remarkable continuity of Spirit reception experiences and effects.

He also returns to the Paul/Luke relationship which I used to introduce the innovation of Wimber's approach, namely his "both/and" conclusion.

---

[116]Ibid., 310.
[117]Ibid., 313.
[118]Ibid., 317.

Such findings also reinforce the difference between how Luke and Paul use Holy Spirit baptism language. This observation has long been posited by many biblical scholars who have come before (such as Fee, Stronstad, Cho, Menzies, etc.). This is not to suggest that Luke and Paul are in contradiction with one another; instead, they clearly had different levels of theological training and development. Both Paul and Luke each have a distinctive voice and contribution to Christian theology that we need to hear and respect.[119]

FOR REFLECTION

This last statement reintroduces the question I raised at the beginning. If Luke has a "distinctive voice and contribution" to Christian theology, then he does function as a theologian, not merely as a descriptive historian. How then should we nuance Luke as both historian *and* theologian? Here I want to make some suggestions, and then hopefully leave the topic for further discussion in the "third wave" and "post-Wimber" tradition.

Perhaps the place to begin is to reflect on the nature of biblical inspiration. In my *Biblical Interpretation 101* I define biblical inspiration as intentional.

> It is important to understand what inspiration does and does not mean. Much could be said about this, but an essential point is that Scripture is inspired in what it intends to say. This is the concept of intentional inspiration.[120]

> The bible is … primarily a set of books that speak to the relationship between God and his people. There are two Testaments, or covenants. To speak of covenant is to speak of a relationship. In this relationship the primary party is God. Therefore, Scripture is primarily revelation from God about himself. This is the intended subject of Scripture.

> Often, because God relates to humanity in and through history, Scripture is concerned with the acts of God in history and

---

[119]Ibid., 318.

[120]Derek Morphew, *Biblical Interpretation 101*, Cape Town: Vineyard International Publishing, Second Edition, 2019, 26.

consequently has an historical interest. Our relationship with God takes places in an environment, in the garden, in nature, in creation, so it has something to say about nature. Man lives in society, so Scripture has something to say about human society. Scripture, however, does not intend to be a purely historical narrative, or a textbook on geology or biology or sociology. When interpreters use Scripture as if it were one of the latter, they misconstrue its intended meaning. It does not intend to make inspired or authoritative statements about geology or sociology. It does intend to make inspired and authoritative statements about humanity in relationship with God. When this involves an historical statement, or a statement about the nature of man, then those statements are also inspired, but when Scripture makes an incidental reference to a certain cosmology or cultural view, it reflects the fact that it is also a human document written by fully human people in their human situation.[121]

Scholars who engage in New Testament research do not assume the inspiration of Scripture. However, when we begin to make theological deductions from Scripture, we generally do assume inspiration. Based on historical research, there is an argument to be made for Luke's purely historical interest. But the moment we engage in theological deductions, this becomes precarious.

But there is a problem even when it comes to a purely historical-critical perspective. In *The Mission of the Kingdom* I trace the primary themes that run like a thread through Luke-Acts. These arise when one uses the redactional approach, which compares Luke and his sources (Mark and Q). It reveals Luke's *tendenz*,[122] or editorial inclinations, and these in turn reveal his theological intent. I have summarized them into one dense statement.

> The new or messianic age has dawned, fulfilling Old Testament expectations and inaugurating the relentless and determined will of God. Its focus is the messianic King, Jesus who, by the power of the Spirit, brings healing and salvation to all nations. This salvation includes previously excluded groups: sinners, the sick, Gentiles, Samaritans, the poor, women and children. It spreads through the proclamation of the word, healing and phenomena of power and

---

[121] Ibid., 27.

[122] A dominating point of view or purpose influencing the structure and content of a literary work, Merriam-Webster dictionary.

revelation. Those who receive this salvation experience forgiveness of sins and respond with song, praise, prayer and wonder. The message has financial and social implications.[123]

In tracing each of these themes, the most comprehensive one is the work of the Spirit.

If the intervention of the rule of God is personified in Jesus, it is executed by the power of the Holy Spirit. There is complete scholarly consensus that this is a major Lucan theme.

The work of the Spirit is probably the most comprehensive aspect of Luke's theology because it spans the period from before the birth of John and Jesus to the later moments of Paul's ministry. Its span is therefore greater than the story of Jesus. However, everything he says about the Spirit is linked to Jesus, or witnesses to Jesus. The Holy Spirit is indeed, to use his words, the "Spirit of Jesus". The terms "Holy Spirit" and "Spirit of Jesus" are used synonymously in Acts 16:6-7.[124]

Embedded in Luke's primary theme is that the gift of the Spirit is the Spirit of prophecy.

That Luke wrote intentionally and wanted to communicate his own "take" is underlined by two further features.

First, the way he structures his content is quite masterful. One can see this from the infancy narrative, where he creates two parallel narratives on John the Baptist and Jesus, but to show the superiority of the latter. It is evident from the carefully balanced parallels between Luke and Acts. It is evident in the way Acts 1:8 (Jerusalem/Judea, Samaria, the ends of the earth) defines the structure of Acts that follows, in three sections. These are only some of his structural intensions.[125]

Second, his formal introduction to Luke (Luke 1:1-4) fuses two interests, the historical and the theological. He writes about his historical research ("carefully investigated everything from the beginning") but describes the events to be narrated as having been "fulfilled among us." This term reflects one of his major themes, namely fulfillment, which is central to his theology.

---

[123]Derek Morphew, *The Mission of the Kingdom: The Theology of Luke*, 31.
[124]Ibid., 49.
[125]Ibid., 98-102.

There are many other points that could be cited to show that Luke wrote with clear theological intensions and ability.

Then, drawing closer to our topic here, there are the obvious signs that Luke has portrayed the Day of Pentecost as a moment of prophetic empowerment and as a succession narrative. We covered this in a previous chapter. Luke has not just told the story of Pentecost. He has theologised the story of Pentecost.

All the above must be born in mind when the notion of Luke writing with a purely historically descriptive perspective is considered.

Yet, as Thomas has shown, and as Wimber noted much earlier, there is "no discernible pattern or formula for how the Spirit falls on us."[126] One cannot press Luke-Acts into a doctrine of subsequence or the norm of tongues as evidence. Neither can one collapse the cases of Spirit reception into conversion/initiation. This position has the least support of all (also refuted by the cases of Jesus and Paul).

It also remains true that Luke has described various Spirit reception events, and in doing so, he reflects his historical sources.

Are we then faced with the "riddle" of Luke as historian *and* theologian? I would like to suggest that there is a solution to this riddle.

In his thesis, Thomas goes to considerable length to justify the interdisciplinary connection between Acts and the later history of revivals using social-scientific tools. His work is thorough and persuasive.[127] However, theologically speaking, there is a more profound justification for this connection, namely the kingdom of God. The Day of Pentecost is described by Luke as an eschatological event, the moment when the long-awaited expectation of the return of the Spirit of prophecy was fulfilled. As I argue in *Breakthrough*, a comprehension of the kingdom of God as inaugurated eschatology leads to a series of implications, one of which is that the history of revivals is the history of repeat Pentecost's, or repeated in-breakings of the kingdom of God.[128] That is why it is valid to "read back" the phenomena of later revivals to help explain Luke's descriptions of Spirit reception.

This is also the key to penetrating Luke's theological assumptions. While Luke reflects his own editorial "take" on his sources, my view is that his theological framework is closer to the eschatological framework of

---

[126]Wimber already cited above.

[127]Lyons, 41-89.

[128]*Breakthrough*, 129-138.

Jesus that many scholars allow, particularly in showing the pivotal influence of Isaiah.[129]

Another commonly accepted view of Luke is the strong influence of the Old Testament, through the Greek Septuagint translation. Despite some sections showing possible Hebrew sources (for instance, the infancy narratives), they have all been thoroughly reworked with the "varnish" of Luke's Greek grammar, which is Septuagintal in style. He is influenced, not only by the style of the Septuagint, but by the Old Testament theology of the Spirit. To understand Luke, one must follow the theology from the Old Testament, into intertestamental expectations of the return of the Spirit, to Luke-Acts (where Jesus as the model of Spirit reception is key), to the history of revivals.

In that trajectory, the centre of everything is the God who comes. The name Yahweh represents the fact that God becomes present.[130] When he becomes present, there is both theophany and prophetic empowering (usually not at the same time). His becoming present is the intervention of his rule. The God who comes is the God to sets up his will on earth, as it is in heaven, often through signs and wonders. When God becomes present in moments of Holy Spirit outpouring, the kingdom of God breaks in through a series of eschatological events. As we traced earlier, there are a whole series of moments when the kingdom became present, from the infancy narratives to Pentecost and beyond. There are also multiple works of the Spirit, matching the multifaceted in-breakings of the kingdom of God.

Is our problem with penetrating Luke's theological intension not based on our Protestant evangelical lenses, which cause us to look for the order of salvation, the *ordo salutis*? What if Luke's theological assumptions were based on kingdom eschatology. When God becomes present in manifest power, something Thomas describes in all the revivals, those who have not yet come to faith and those who are already disciples of Jesus experience it differently. When a non-believer walks into the "power zone" that becomes present in times of revival, they experience dramatic conversions. When disciples of Jesus walk into such a space, they are prophetically empowered for witness. Because revivals are primary times when God visits his church, most of the Spirit reception phenomena are prophetic

---

[129]In *The Mission of the Kingdom* I argue that the dawning of the messianic era is more fundamental to Luke than salvation, 33-34.

[130]*Breakthrough*, 19-101.

empowering. But all revivals have non-believers walking in.

That is why, as I describe above, there is a spectrum of ways in which we experience the Spirit. There are "simultaneous" people, "subsequence" people, many fillings people, and various combinations of them. This is precisely what Thomas finds in his revivals research. "For some, the dramatic encounter with the Spirit of God is what initiated their conversion while others report having been believers for years before experiencing the Spirit so dramatically."[131]

But none of this is because Luke is only being historically descriptive, it is a reflection of the trajectory from the Old Testament, through Luke-Acts and into the history of revivals, which is the theology of the kingdom of God. Luke is intentionally writing theology as well. This is important from the perspective of a charismatic theology. Luke is *the* primary New Testament inspired writer to provide us with the work of the Spirit as prophetic empowering. As Thomas noted, his theological contribution must be valued, alongside that of Paul and John.

Wimber's formative insights have been further nuanced by Thomas's valuable contribution.

---

[131]Lyons, 310.

PART TWO: THE GIFTS OF THE SPIRIT

By Øyvind Nerheim

As with Part One, this is not a mere repeat of Wimber's teaching. It is a careful examination of Wimber's teaching in the light of Scripture and in relation to other views held by his contemporaries. Øyvind does not agree with Wimber on every point, and explains where he things his reading of a given biblical text is not correct, or not likely.

In order to position Wimber in the wider context, Øyvind examines literature in the Norwegian and English languages, and surveys the viewpoints of evangelical, Pentecostal and charismatic writers and teachers.

Overall, he articulates and supports Wimber's fundamental teaching.

INTRODUCTION

ACTUALITY, RELEVANCE, AND MOTIVATION

The greatest advantages of Wimber's theology of spiritual gifts are its ability to lower the doorstep into charismatic ministry, the fact that it opens up for focus on developing gifts, and the comfort and relief it can provide for people who think they have "lost" the spiritual gift they believed they had.

My motivation for writing this thesis is twofold. First, I have seen and experienced how the Vineyard setting and approach to ministry managed to lower the doorstep into ministry and let everybody "play." The second part of my motivation is personal; A few years ago, I was seriously troubled because a specific gift I once "had," apparently ceased to function. This bothered me until I came across Wimber's dynamic understanding of spiritual gifts, and I realized that the Lord had needed me to function in that gift for a while, but now needed me to function in other gifts.

I found that Wimber's dynamic model provides a very solid and adequate methodological basis for teaching on "development of gifts." Compared to models that are more static, the gracelet-ministry-gifted equipper (office) model provides an excellent framework for development since growth in frequency and effect is the core of the model. Based on Wimber's model, the various tools and models for development I presented in Chapter 9 can serve as helpful means for facilitating the future development of gracelets into ministries and further into gifted equippers (offices).

A dynamic view of spiritual gifts does also have strong implications for pastoral counseling. Adoption of a dynamic understanding of one's gifting can be a great comfort for people who have lost the spiritual gift they believed they had been given to keep and use for the rest of their life. It is easy to come under condemnation for misuse or neglect of the gift if one's theology says one has owned the gift and that God must have removed the gift since it is no longer active. Teaching based on Wimber's dynamic model can help the person to understand that God now might have a different kind of ministry he or she now needs to focus on.

A central part of the foundation of this thesis is the "punctual" aspect of the aorist Paul is using when describing the various gifts.[132] Are spiritual gifts primarily something to possess, or are they given through the believer by the Holy Spirit when He lets him or her function in a gift or anointing? Wimber's theology of spiritual gifts forces us to investigate whether the punctual aspect is the key to understand Paul's description of the early church's experience of spiritual gifts. Karl Inge Tangen argues from his research on Christian healing that this question is fundamental with regard to the question whether all Christians can operate in the gift of healing—which is his area of study.[133] This is of equal importance for most other spiritual gifts.

Wimber has developed a theology of *charismata* which is distinguished by its dynamic characteristic. This is foremost expressed in his notion of development of spiritual gifts from "gracelets" to "ministries" and to "gifted equippers (offices)." The central focus of this thesis is to "present, analyze and evaluate John Wimber's theology of *charismata*, with particular emphasis on its punctual and dynamic aspects and its use in the Vineyard movement". Key questions I will explore are:

1. What is Wimber's theology of *charismata*?

2. Was Wimber's model useful for ministry in Vineyard-churches in California?

3. Are Wimber's theology of spiritual gifts in general and particularly its dynamic aspects compatible with the intention of Paul's texts?

4. What implications does the model have for the development of gift-based ministry?

SURVEY OF VINEYARD PASTORS IN CALIFORNIA

To evaluate of the usefulness of Wimber's theology I wanted to find out

---

[132]Since this word can have a variety of meanings, I will define the way I am using it in this thesis as "limited to a specific point in time." "Instantaneous," "momentarily," and "spontaneous" are to a certain degree synonyms.

[133]Karl Inge Tangen, 1993, 107.

whether his own movement has embraced it and found it useful over time. To research this I conducted a survey (in 1999) among the Vineyard pastors in California, where Wimber lived and served.

I found that many of the Vineyard pastors preferred to use Wimber's set of labels: "gracelet, ministry, gifted equipper (office)," and many of the pastors regarded Wimber's division between "gracelets" and "ministries" as Biblical and useful, but many of the pastors replied that they preferred to organize the gifts as "natural" or "supernatural." Almost all the pastors saw spiritual gifts as "given through the believer for the present situation," and many of the pastors emphasized the situational aspects when they taught on spiritual gifts. All the pastors thought that all believers can expect to see people they pray for get healed, and many of the pastors had a positive experience with releasing the church to minister in all the gifts. Most of the pastors primarily encouraged people to be "open for the Holy Spirit to give them any gracelet or let them work in his power whenever the situation requires it." It is most surprising to find that only half of the pastors demonstrated that they understood Wimber's model and grasped the concept of "gracelets."

I therefore concluded that the Vineyard movement—at least in California—did adopted Wimber's theology of *charismata*, but the dynamic concept of "gracelets" had not been grasped by all. The objects of this survey were Vineyard pastors in California, which means the group who had had easiest access to Wimber's teaching. This group had the best opportunity to see Wimber teach and practice his theology in practice. I will therefore give this weight in the evaluation of Wimber's theology of *charismata*. The drawback of limiting this survey to California is the lack of data from Vineyard pastors in other countries. It would have been interesting to analyze how Wimber's theology of *charismata* has been adopted and used in various cultures. I can therefore only offer a few comments on the issue of cross-cultural transferability.

CROSS-CULTURAL TRANSFERABILITY

Are any foundational assumptions or aspects of Wimber's dynamic theology of *charismata* culturally dependent on the suburban Southern Californian culture? Are the practical manifestations of his theology transferable and useful in for instance the Norwegian culture, or will the somewhat static and introverted characteristic of the Norwegian self-understanding hinder this? I will now look briefly at these issues, mainly by relating to a couple of Vineyard leaders.

The Californian culture can be described as laidback and casual, and Californians are generally more open to social interaction with strangers, something which makes it easier to e.g. share a encouraging word of knowledge with a stranger. This aspect certainly has a lot to do with dynamic ministry in *charismata*, but not with the dynamic parts of Wimber's model, only with how gifts are used. I do not think that the Californian culture is a prerequisite for people to casually minister ad-hoc in various new gifts. Hans Sundberg, who was the leader of the Vineyard in the Nordic nations, saw the danger of Vineyard people misunderstanding the Californian culture to be what we should import.

> It is a problem with our, e.g. the Nordic perspective (= the common culture that the five Nordic nations have), common understanding of what is okay to be and to do in our own setting—and the challenge that John Wimber gave us in his teaching about power evangelism. The laid-back Californian style and the Nordic culture can seem to be total opposites. And when people in "Wimberized" settings take the Californian style to be *the* way a Spirit-led ministry should work it creates a problem. Wimber never intended to export a Californian culture. And we in our nations shouldn't treat his challenge to be a bold Nordic people outside our cultural settings. So my answer is yes—*our* understanding of being a dynamic people of God can easily be mixed up with being Californian laid-back. We have to break out of that and be bold Nordic Spirit-led people.[134]

Another aspect is the Scandinavian focus on permanency, stability, and safety, which stand in contrast e.g. to the high job-changing rate in California. This suggests that it is harder for a Norwegian to change his identity from being, for instance, an evangelist, to focus on administration if the ministry needs around him change. I believe that this is just as hard for Americans due to their strong focus on titles and official status.

Gregg Shaw, an American missionary who has served in several cultures, relates, "the Norwegian culture's strong emphasis on democratic values is coherent with John Wimber's emphasis on 'everybody gets to

---

[134]Sundberg, 2002.

play'." On the other hand he has noticed that the upper parts of Wimber's model—ministry/gifted equipper (office)—can conflict with the "Jante-law."[135] He sees this aspect of the Scandinavian culture as a parallel to the Australian "tall poppy syndrome" (the tallest poppy is the one who gets his head cut of). He thinks these "laws" manifests themselves in attitudes like "there are no real prophets, or evangelists, or apostles".[136] The Jante-law applies also to the personal level, discouraging anybody from thinking he is e.g. a prophet.

---

[135]The Law of Jante is a code of conduct known in Nordic countries that characterizes not conforming, doing things out of the ordinary, or being overtly personally ambitious as un-worthy and inappropriate. There are ten rules in the law as defined by Aksel Sandemose (*A Fugitive Crosses His Tracks*, 1933) all expressive of variations on a single theme and usually referred to as a homogeneous unit: You are not to think you're anyone special or that you're better than us.

[136]Shaw, 2002.

1: WIMBER'S THEOLOGY OF *CHARISMATA*

This chapter is a presentation of Wimber's theology of *charismata*. I will use other sources to put Wimber in context. By including quotes of theologians from both the Third Wave/Vineyard camp and other camps, I hope to provide a basis for understanding Wimber, as well as to demonstrate that these issues are the subject to serious scholarship.

The presentation of Wimber's view is based on the booklets and tapes developed for the "Spiritual Gifts Seminar" in 1985. Since this is the only comprehensive teaching he published on the subject, I have chosen to base the presentation on this material. It is likely that he developed at least parts of his theology of *charismata* further, but I have not found either evidence or hints of major developments. The only exception is a paper from 1997, which displays a more reserved attitude concerning gifted equippers (offices/titles). This paper was written as a response to the focus on the "five-fold ministry," and "super-Apostles" based on restoration theology. This issue was important to Wimber and central to the scope of this article since,

> this type of thinking also violates a fundamental Vineyard value in that it reduces those outside the special core to a group who exists to receive what the core has to dispense. In other words, a reliance on the special corps of people to dispense the special revelations from God disempowers the church and turns God's army into an audience. Our goal in the Vineyard is to equip the church to be full members in the army of God. "Everyone can play" (that is participate).[137]

---

[137]Wimber, 1997b, 5. All Wimber's pastoral letters, or "Reflections" are now published in

THEOLOGICAL POSITION

Jim Packer describes what he calls "Wimber's theories" as a series of affirmations: "the triune God continues," "God's continues," "miracles continue," "the revelatory work of the Holy Spirit continues." Concerning the first statement, he, with Wimber, asks "evangelicals, who habitually insist that they alone do full Biblical justice to the second person of the Godhead, Jesus Christ our Lord: are you also doing full Biblical justice to the third person, the Holy Spirit?" He concludes about Wimber, "to honor the Holy Spirit by expecting more, and attempting more, than was usual, was from one perspective the whole thrust of his ministry".[138]

The theological basis for much of Wimber's teaching is Ladd's theology of the Kingdom of God as both present and futuristic—already and not yet. This is the basis for his emphasis of charismatic phenomena like healing, signs and wonders, power-encounters, and hearing God's voice. Another characteristic element in Wimber's theology was his strong emphasis on followership. He saw the life and ministry of Jesus as a model of how to live as followers,[139] depending on God as Jesus depended on the Father (John 5:19). Wimber emphasized, "Jesus relied on the promptings from the Holy Spirit for his ministry," and made the case that he "performed these works of power as a human being, led by the Holy Spirit (see e.g. Luke 4:1, 14, 5:17)".[140] This makes Jesus relevant as a model for life and ministry, and is an important part of the foundation for Wimber's focus on equipping all the saints to do the ministry of Jesus.

The church's task in following Jesus is therefore to expand the kingdom by calling people to conversion and making disciples of them.[141] The ministry of the church in the world today is the ministry of Jesus, and should be modeled after Jesus' own life and ministry. Olsen suggests that Wimber's overemphasis on the supernatural aspects of this ministry is due to the church's negligence of this aspect.[142]

"Signs and Wonders" is a phrase many connect with Wimber and the

---

Derek Morphew, *John Wimber's Pastoral Letters*, 2020.

[138]Packer in Pytches, 1998, 261.

[139]Olsen, 1989, 10.

[140]Nathan in Pytches, 1998, 96. This statement is not meant in any way to take away from Jesus' full divinity or to teach some kenotic theory of the Incarnation.

[141]Wimber, 1992, 76.

[142]Ibid., 18.

Vineyard movement, due to Wimber's books *Power Healing* and *Power Evangelism*, as well as the many healing and renewal conferences hosted by the movement. D. A. Carson states "the distinction of the Vineyard movement does not lie in its prayers for the sick but in its insistence that signs and wonders must be part of normal Christianity".[143] Based on this demand he thinks the Vineyard has put too high expectations upon itself. He suspects that healing occurs "considerably less frequent [than reported] in the Vineyard." He goes on to share a thought that is relevant to the topic of this thesis:

> The Vineyard movement seems to have focused on the relatively peripheral [gifts] (namely, the kinds of phenomena found in 1 Corinthians 12–14 and some other passages), called them "signs and wonders," and elevated them to a place of central importance.[144]

It seems like he includes most spiritual gifts in this "signs and wonders" category and limits the gifts to function as signs ad wonders. Throughout this presentation of Wimber's theology of *charismata*, we will see that Wimber does not limit spiritual gifts to signs and wonders.

Wimber's starting point concerning *charismata* is the prophecy in Joel 2:28–29. He writes that,

> Since the beginning, the Spirit has desired to find those through whom he could manifest himself. . . . Genesis1:2, . . . Num.11:26–30, . . . Joel.2:28–29, . . . In Acts 2:14–21, Peter says that the day which was prophesied by Joel had arrived. We now live in that day and God is ministering the gracelets to those who desire them.[145]

---

[143]Carson, 1992, 111. David F. Weels, *God the Evangelist,* 1987, 87, addressed the question of "whether it is right to expect 'signs and wonders' to accompany the preaching of the gospel." This was written on the basis of the Consultation of the Work of the Holy Spirit and Evangelization in Oslo in 1985, where John Wimber attended. He asks and analyzes if "signs and wonders" are "predictable concomitants to the fullness of the Spirit? [or] concomitants only to the apostolic gifted equipper (office) and role, . . . or . . . periodically realized in the life of the church and thus not predictable concomitants?"
[144]Ibid., 113.
[145]Wimber, 1985c, 1.

A HISTORICAL SHIFT FROM "BAPTISM IN THE SPIRIT" TO "ANOINTING"

The Vineyard has been a part of what church historians calls "the Third Wave." Winson Synan suggests that the Third Wave

> may have represented the reaction of the churches to . . . the increasing numbers of Christian laypersons leaving these [the Catholic and Protestant] churches and joining Pentecostal and independent churches. . . . As more churches opened up to freer and more "charismatic" worship, fewer members were likely to desert their local churches.[146]

Perhaps the most distinguished doctrine in the prior "waves" was the doctrine of "baptism in the Spirit." Together with the Pentecostal practice of re-baptizing this was incompatible with evangelical theology and could not be "brought along."

Third wavers do not teach a crisis experience of baptism in the Holy Spirit subsequent to conversion, and they see tongues as only one of the many gifts of the Spirit.[147]

In contrast to many charismatic leaders' inclination to be the center of attention, "was Wimber's evident desire to 'equip the saints,' . . . to enable others to minister in the power of the Holy Spirit".[148] Wright believes that a part of the explanation of the Vineyard movement's impact was

> its shift away from the theological categories of Pentecostalism in search for more dynamic paradigms for the Spirit's work. The contested phrase "baptism in the Spirit" was gradually displaced by the more flexible notion of "anointing." Gifts of the Spirit were not limited in number and not the possession of the individual, rather they were dynamically given according to situation and need. The focus was placed upon the intimacy of the believer's relationship with the Spirit who enables, rather than proof of ownership of gifts.[149]

This historical analysis of the Vineyard demonstrates clearly the important role Wimber's dynamic theology of *charismata* has played in terms of the

---

[146]Winson Synan, 1997, 274.

[147]Ibid., 285.

[148]Wright, 1995, 72.

[149]Ibid., 72.

Vineyard's profile and expansion.

OVERVIEW OF WIMBER'S THEOLOGY OF *CHARISMATA*

The central dynamic of Wimber's theology of *charismata* is described through this slogan: "God can use any of the gracelets through any of his people whenever he wants." This theology is based on the nearness and availability of the Kingdom of God, and spiritual gifts are seen as "concrete manifestations of the Spirit".[150] Packer's description of Wimber's ministry as a "naturally supernatural ministry"[151] pinpoints Wimber's attitude towards supernatural spiritual gifts, describing that Wimber saw them as a part of everyday life and wanted to avoid any "hype" or exaltation of strong gifts. This is exemplified by the general rule practiced in most Vineyard churches not to announce prophecies by "thus says the Lord," but with humble awareness of the fact that not even the strongest prophets can avoid coloring their presentations, as well as the freedom to test everything. Wagner says Wimber "wanted to avoid the phenomenon of superstar healers and instead involve the whole Body in the ministry of healing".[152]

Wimber defined spiritual gifts like this:

> The gifts (*charismata*) or gracelets of the Holy Spirit are transrational manifestations of God. They are given by God for the purpose of ministry taking place for the good of the body of Christ.[153]

A few years later, he offered this definition as a summary of a teaching on the releasing of the gifts in the church:

> The gifts of the Spirit are God's supernatural expressions of love, caring, kindness, healing, and concern—bestowed upon us and through us.[154]

I will come back to the word "gracelets" below. With a broader scope, Wimber called spiritual gifts "the expression of God's power at work in the

---

[150]Hunter, 1999.
[151]Packer in Pytches, 1998, 267.
[152]Packer, 1996, 39.
[153]Wimber, 1985a, 8.
[154]Wimber, 1991, 159.

world (Church) today".[155] Based on Mel Robeck he wrote that,

> The source of the gifts is the Holy Spirit. The recipients are the Community of the Spirit, sometimes called the People of God or the Body of Christ. The essence of the gifts is manifestations of grace. Their purpose is to edify the Body, equip the saints, and glorify God. Their motive should always be love.[156]

However, Wimber did not limit the use of *charismata* to the "prayer meetings" that were so popular in charismatic circles in the 70s and 80s. Compared to the Pentecostal and charismatic movements' focus on Acts and the Pauline literature and the relative neglect of the Gospels, Wimber "dusted off the Gospels and allowed them to challenge our preconceptions about the supernatural world and the power of the Holy Spirit".[157] Jesus modeled exercising gifts in the public square. Examples of this are the woman caught in adultery (prophecy exercised), the woman at the well (word of knowledge or prophecy exercised), and Nathanael (word of knowledge exercised), not to mention the many healings and deliverances. One of Wimber's mottoes was: "the meat is in the streets."

Nathan points out that,

> Wimber's perspective on Jesus' use of spiritual gifts prompted many Christians to seek to exercise gifts of the Holy Spirit not only in the church meetings, but also in the opportunities for ministry at work, in their neighborhoods, at school and in the wider community.[158]

To give a balanced picture, I will now explore a few specific aspects of Wimber's theology of *charismata*.

THE RIGHT MOTIVATION FOR MINISTRY

Since I have not focused a lot on Wimber's general theology of *charismata*, I have included an extensive quote to provide a broad picture of how he saw spiritual gifts in relationship to the rest of his theology and to the gospel itself.

---

[155] Wimber, 1985c, 1.
[156] Ibid., 1.
[157] Nathan in Pytches, 1998, 96.
[158] Ibid, 97-98.

The mercy of God is manifested and demonstrated in human form, even as Jesus Christ the incarnate God came that we may have an understanding of the love of God, he is now giving you the opportunity as the body of Christ to do the same work as he did. A gushing forth of the love of God, healing, preaching of the word, counsel, embracing of children, healing of the blind. Every place Jesus went he ministered to the people at the point of their need, their situation. As he was always ministering the love of his father we are to do that today, because he lives in us. . . . And in so doing the gifts will be manifest in us, and the help that we need to express that love in an unqualified way, a really committed way, a powerful way, will be right with us—the very presence of the Holy Spirit. . . . Not thinking too highly of himself, he left the father, he came and became man, so that you and I could relate to him, he saved us by the shedding of his blood and his coming to Calvary. You might be the only Jesus somebody meets between now and eternity. You and I are to be the very hand of Jesus. Be prepared to give the gifts he gives to you.[159]

It is clear from this quote that Wimber saw spiritual gifts as an integral part of the presentation of the gospel—demonstrating the love of God. He did not see the exercising of spiritual gifts as an exotic charismatic privilege, but simply as an expression of God's love.

Wimber was disturbed by the people who question his decision to step away from being Senior Pastor of a large church, and suggested that whether a person takes a demotion in the same spirit as a promotion is a good humility test. He underlined that,

all ministries are (should be) exercised in humility and with love for the whole Body. It's not just important what we do, but it's equally important how we exercise these "services," or "*diakonias*." At times there seems to be more emphasis on the gifts of the Spirit than on the Fruit of the Spirit. All the ministries should be exercised in fair, even handed treatment of people.[160]

This attitude is expressed in this quote:

I don't mind what I do, just so I have a piece of Jesus' kingdom work. I'm change in God's pocket. He can spend me anyway he wants. I

---

[159]Wimber, 1985d, Tape2.
[160]Wimber, 1997b, 10.

joined up with nothing, and I intend to go out with nothing but Jesus.[161]

THE GRACELETS AND THE KINGDOM

Wimber's understanding of the Kingdom of God was based on Ladd's theology. He described it as,

> the invasion of God's rulership into the domain of Satan. When Jesus came, war was declared. It is a cosmic war! The war was won in the death, resurrection, and ascension of Jesus. We now live "between the times." The war is won but the battles continue. In these ongoing battles, God gives us gracelets, along with the armor of Ephesians 6, to help wage war. We are called to be an army, not an audience. In the battles which lie before us God will deliver his gracelets at the most advantageous time to help win.[162]

He continued by giving a few examples of how he pictured this might work.[163]

> Gracelets are the tools God gives us to fight the good fight. Let us allow his "dancing hand" to grace us. Let us be active soldiers in his army. Let us win all the battles we can.[164]

The way Wimber believed we should fight the war corresponds to the commission Jesus gave to the twelve disciples to "Preach this message; 'the Kingdom of heaven is near.' Heal the sick, raise the dead, cleanse those who have leprosy, drive out demons" (Matthew 10:7–8). Nathan writes: "Wimber taught that Jesus not only taught and preached the message of the Kingdom, but that he also demonstrated it with works of power".[165] The same authority given to the seventy-two (Luke 10.1, 8–16) was given to every believer. Wimber's greatest desire and ministry objective was to see all believers equipped to utilize their potential.

Derek Morphew lays out the basis of the theology of the Kingdom of

---

[161]Ibid., 10.
[162]Wimber, 1985c, 6.
[163]These are included in the descriptions of each *charisma* in Chapter 3.
[164]Ibid., 6.
[165]Nathan in Pytches, 1998, 101.

God in his book *Breakthrough*.[166] He points out three main demonstrations/picture of the Kingdom in the Old Testament: the power clash of the Exodus event, the Davidic monarchy, and the Prophetic promise.

We find an important picture of the Kingdom in the description of Solomon's table (1 Kings 4). Key words are multiplication, party time/feast, abundance, shalom, power, and practical wisdom. The book of Isaiah is saturated with this new promise; it tells of how Yahweh will come as the Davidic Messiah—descended from David but far greater, and of how the Spirit will gush forward as rivers. The salvation that will come is characterized by healing, forgiveness, liberation, Shalom, and resurrection. The content of the promise is a new people, a new Jerusalem, a new heaven and a new earth, and the judgement of evil.[167]

IMPARTATION

The first theme I will look at is how one receives spiritual gifts. Even though Wimber underlined that the *charismata* are spontaneously given by the Holy Spirit, this was balanced by his teaching on impartation, i.e. how the *charismata* are given and received. He emphasizes two aspects, which can seem contradictory at first sight:

1. Impartation is a sovereign act of God.

2. Gifts and mantles can be passed on by the laying on of hands. 2 Timothy 1:6b is the central Pauline passage where we find an example of impartation by laying on of hands: "the gift of God, which is in you through the laying on of my hands."

The Laying on of Hands to Pass on a Mantle

Wimber lists several examples of people in the Bible who received their gifted equipper (office) and mantle for ministry through the laying on of the hands of their mentor or master. Joshua received his mantle from Moses (Deuteronomy 34:9), Timothy from the elders, and the seven deacons from the twelve disciples (Acts 6:7). He also includes an example of a mantle being given by someone who did not have it—Anannias who was no

---

[166]Derek Morphew, *Breakthrough: Discovering the Kingdom, 5th Edition*, 2019.
[167]Ibid., 19-101.

apostle, laid his hands on Paul, to be an apostle (Acts 9:10, 17).[168]

Wimber emphasizes that it is important to pay attention to 1 Timothy 5:22 ("do not be hasty") when passing on your mantle and blessing.[169] He built it into the Vineyard culture as a strong value not to rush to lay hands on people to install them into gifted equippers (offices). Titles are not given to people before they have demonstrated their character and ministry. Even people with proven gifts and ministry from another setting need to prove effective and anointed in the new role. Call and gift are not equal. Wimber believed, "the Lord doesn't want theatre or show, only humble servants. . . . If you have a call: keep your mouth shut about it and just do it!" Sundberg says that Wimber leaned back to his Quaker roots in his last years. He had seen how titles could corrupt the function of gifted people. He disliked the way people (and gifts/manifestations) were given titles and stage focus in the Toronto movement (2004). He emphasized that in the New Covenant, there is only one mentality to be passed on, Jesus' mentality.

A Sovereign Act

Wimber's starting point is that the distribution of *charismata* is a sovereign act by God. He states, "God can move to give gracelets, ministries, and gifted equippers (offices) as he desires",[170] and lists Acts 2:1–4, 4:13, and 10:44 as references.

Wimber resisted attempts to standardize spiritual experiences. He held that Acts cannot be used as a basis for the doctrine of baptism in the Holy Spirit with speaking in tongues as a mandatory sign of the filling of the Holy Spirit, subsequent to conversion.[171]

Wimber held this position based on two observations: first because the order varies, and secondly because the sign varies. By comparing three conversion-stories in Acts, we see that the order of events does not follow a special agenda. The people in Cornelius' house first received the Holy Spirit and were baptized later (Acts 10:47), the people in Samaria had been baptized but had not received the Holy Spirit (Acts 8:15, as well as

---

[168]Wimber, 1985b, 5.
[169]Ibid., 5.
[170]Wimber, 1985c, 4.
[171]Wimber, Anaheim, 1991.

19:1ff),[172] but the normal pattern was to receive the Holy Spirit when baptized.[173] Concerning the sign that accompanies reception of the Holy Spirit, Wimber gives three examples: The disciples were first "filled" with the Holy Spirit at Pentecost with fire and wind and tongues as signs (Acts 2:2f), and again in Acts 4:31 when the sign was shaking of the place they were in. Wimber summarizes the Spirit's activity in Acts by quoting Hummel.

> The Spirit "fell on" (three times); "came upon" (twice); and was "poured out" (twice) as recorded in Acts. The believers "received" (twice); were "filled with the Holy Spirit" (five times) as noted in Acts. The results were observable in speaking in tongues (three times); preaching (three times); and the anointing to witness with power (twice).[174]

Fillings of the Spirit or Baptism in the Spirit

Regarding the question of when such a baptism in the Spirit takes place, Wimber believed it is "initiatory and repeatable".[175] He thought that this was a question of labels. He agreed with Spittler that "a synonym [for baptism in the Spirit] which may be helpful is the word 'overwhelm'".[176]

The Spirit's coming to the disciples at Pentecost anointed them for their function in the unfolding story of redemptive history. Initial and repeated fillings empowered them for a prophetic ministry (compare Acts 2:4 with 4:31. Peter was filled on both occasions). No single event in the book of Acts will provide the model for the sequence of an individual's repentance, faith, water baptism, and the empowerment of the Spirit. The pattern, if there is one, is that the Spirit blows where he wants.[177]

Contrary to Pentecostal theology, Wimber was therefore arguing that

---

[172]Without entering into the discussion I will mention that some hold that it is possible that the Samaritans in Acts 8 not had been converted since they "believed Philip" (8:11) and not the gospel itself.

[173]"From Acts 2 onward the gift of the Spirit is normally attached to conversion-initiation, and why the suspension of the Spirit from baptism (as at Acts 8) is regarded as an anomaly to be corrected as soon as possible", Turner, 1998, 352.

[174]Hummel, 1978, 108 in Wimber, 1985c, 4.

[175]Wimber, 1985c, 4.

[176]Spittler, 1982 and Vine, 1940, 97 in Wimber 1985c, 4.

[177]Ibid., 4.

speaking in tongues does not have to go together with baptism or filling of the Holy Spirit. Max Turner shares this view and states that there is no basis in Paul's writings to "assume that reception of such charismatic gifts as tongues, interpretation, prophecy and gifts of healings, depends on a post-conversion crisis experience of empowering".[178] He argues that the attempt to restrict "*charismata* to a special, 'Spirit-baptized,' group . . . was precisely the Corinthians' misunderstanding." I will come back to this later.[179]

Although impartation is a sovereign act by the Holy Spirit, is it important to point out that impartation of *charismata* happens in the contexts of ministry. Wimber underlined the importance of not "confusing the gift of the Spirit with the gifts (gracelets) of the Spirit," and wrote that "The actualization of the Spirit which empowers one for service occurs when ministry needs to take place. The gifts of the Spirit are the tools which come with the empowering to fulfill the ministry required".[180]

Based on Acts 1:8 Wimber states that the purpose of baptism in the Spirit "is to be empowered by the Spirit for ministry," and he believed that "fillings with the Spirit for effective witness and service should be normative for all Christians. The disciples fillings are related to service/ministry (Acts 2:4, 4:31, etc.)".[181] Clinton points out, "Spiritual gifts are released and caught in an environment where spiritual power and ministry are happening".[182] He calls this the principle of spiritual contagion. This corresponds closely to Wimber's style and dynamic understanding of impartation. He did not act as if he had a "mechanical" model that only those who he placed his hands on would, and always would, experience an impartation of the gifts Wimber taught and demonstrated.

THE DYNAMIC ASPECTS

The focal element of this presentation of and analysis of Wimber's theology of *charismata* is the concept of a continuum from "gracelets" to "ministries" and to "gifted equippers (offices)." This concept is based on a

---

[178]Turner, 1998, 351.
[179]See Chapter 6, The Pentecostal View.
[180]Wimber, 1985c, 4.
[181]Ibid., 4.
[182]Clinton, 1999.

punctual understanding of *charismata* as manifestations, which I will analyze closer in Chapter 7.

Wimber's teaching is strongly polemic against what he called "The Traditional View." He describes this view as based on a static understanding of the body metaphor in 1 Corinthians 12:14–29, and summarizes it like this: 1)You already have gifts, 2) You need to discover and develop these, 3) You are to be content and not seek any others".[183] I assume that few would identify themselves with the last part of this description. I do not know of anyone who teaches this, but this mindset can often be the result of negligence of encouraging believers to seek "the greater gifts." Perhaps Wimber described this view stereotypically to show how it can prevent people from being open towards the spontaneous promptings or gracelets of the Holy Spirit.

> Many of us have been taught that this list (1 Corinthians 12:8–12) refers to a onetime, permanent endowment for each person. But I believe that Paul is not talking here about a dispensing of permanently held gifts. He is talking about passing touches of the Spirit at different times in different settings. Russell Spittler calls them "gracelets." I like that name. It implies that these are little expressions of God's grace. They come and they go, like fragrant flowers that open and close. In fact, they can come and go in milliseconds. One time a certain gift goes to one person, and another time it goes to another person. At any given time, a person could minister in prophecy, in teaching, in healing, or in some other form of blessing for the good of others.[184]

Wimber saw the exhortations to "eagerly desire gifts" in 1 Corinthians 12–14, as the main problems with this "Traditional View." Instead of using the static "body" model he suggests that the correct interpretative key is "when the body meets together." He lists twelve cases where Paul uses this phrase more-or-less identically: 11:17, 11:18, 11:20, 11:30, 11:33, 11:34, 14:4, 14:5, 14:19, and 14:23.[185]

Wimber writes concerning the word of knowledge that "this gracelet (as well as the others) is not the possession of man to be used at his will".[186]

---

[183]Wimber, 1985a, 8.
[184]Wimber, 1991, 147-8.
[185]Wimber, 1985a, 8.
[186]Wimber, 1985b, 4.

He quotes James Dunn who argues that "it is a particular word given in a particular instance and is 'mine' only in the act and moment of uttering it".[187] Todd Hunter puts it like this "Gifts are not resident in the believer but situational and given on the parameters of the will of God, through the Christian to other people".[188] C. Samuel Storms describes the "Third Wave" position on miraculous gifts. He says "Gifts of healings … are occasional and subject to the purposes of God".[189]

The following statements exemplify central aspects of Wimber's theology, which I will examine in more detail throughout the thesis:

- "Be prepared to give the gifts he gives to you".[190]

- "The Holy Spirit can let anyone work in any gift any time He needs to".[191]

- "The gracelets [are] being used by God through us at a special time and occasion".[192]

- "As God sees fit, his dancing hand anoints (gives a GRACELET to) a believer . . . The GRACELETs are given by the Spirit. As they are used service is effected by the power of God".[193]

- "The believer can move in all spiritual gifts in accordance with God's timing and purpose."

- "A believer does not possess gifts, a believer receives gifts from God to be used at special times for special occasions".[194]

- "When we receive the Holy Spirit, we gain access to all the gifts we need to advance the kingdom of God".[195]

- "The gifts . . . are given to us and through us to use for others".[196]

---

[187]James Dunn, 1975, 221.
[188]Todd Hunter, 1999.
[189]Storms in Grudem, 1996, 213.
[190]Wimber, 1985d, Tape2.
[191]Hunter, 2000.
[192]Wimber, 1985c, 3.
[193]Wimber, 1985b, 3.
[194]Wimber, 1985c, 1.
[195]Wimber, 1987, 200.
[196]Wimber, 1985c, 1.

- "They come and they go, like fragrant flowers that open and close. In fact, they can come and go in milliseconds".[197]

ROLE - GRACELET – MINISTRY – GIFTED EQUIPPER (OFFICE)

Wimber was probably inspired by Wagner's distinction between "role" and "gift" to break down "spiritual gifts" into sub-categories.[198] This table presents a schematized display of how he broke it down at "this point in time".[199] I have not been able to find many indications of whether Wimber developed this further or not, but I suspect "role" became less important to him since he does not mention or highlight it anywhere else.

F1: Schematized Presentation of Role – Gracelet – Ministry - Gifted equipper (office)			
Role	Gracelet/anointing	Ministry	Gifted equipper (office)
witness	evangelism	evangelist	evangelist
teaching	teaching	teacher	
prophecy	prophecy	prophet	prophet
giving	giving	giving	

Wimber used Joel as an example of how one can move from "role" to "gifted equipper (office)." Joel lived in Jerusalem and saw rationally (on the role-level) that "Judah was heading for destruction".[200] On the gracelet/anointing level, "the prophesy of Joel was the anointing of God coming to Joel (1:1) and the speaking of that word by Joel to Judah".[201] Concerning the ministry level Wimber wrote, "We don't know how often Joel was used by God to prophesy. If occasions became frequent, this would have become his ministry, which it most likely did".[202] We can be more certain about the gifted equipper (office) level based on Acts 2:16, "God at some time appointed/called Joel to the gifted equipper (office) of prophet".[203]

I will mostly focus on the "gracelet" level in the continuum (compared

---

[197]Wimber, 1991, 148.
[198]Wagner, 1976a, 75-76, and 1976b, 90-92.
[199]Wimber, 1985c, 2.
[200]Ibid., 2.
[201]Ibid., 2.
[202]Ibid., 3.
[203]Ibid., 3.

to the "role" and "ministry" levels), since this is a unique element in Wimber's theology of *charismata*. As shown in the figure below these words are meant to represent various "levels" of gifting or use of particular *charismata*. The arrows between the circles indicate development/growth in the use of the particular *charismata*. The vertical arrow represents the quality or effect of the gift exercised.

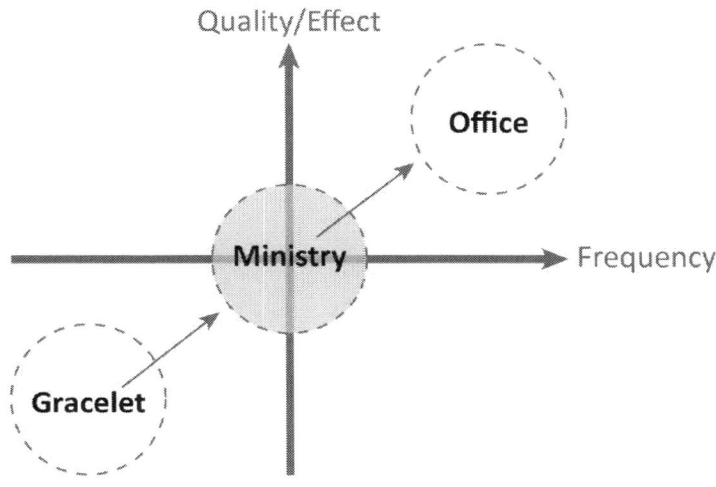

F2: Gracelet – Ministry - Office

This idea of varied quality of spiritual gift-use might seem strange to some readers since God is a giver of perfect gifts (John 1:17),[204] but in Romans 12:6 Paul urges the believer to prophesy in "proportion to his faith." Grudem writes that this "indicates that the gift can be more or less strongly developed in different individuals, or in the same individual over a period of time".[205] He refers to 1 Timothy 4:14, 2 Timothy 1:6, Acts 18:24, 1 Corinthians 12:11, 14:18, and concludes, "spiritual gifts may vary in strength" and explains that this "depends on a combination of divine and human influence".[206] Along the same lines Storms states, concerning prophetic

---

[204]What this text is really saying is that all the gifts that are perfect come from above, not that all gifts that come from above are perfect.

[205]Grudem, 1994, 1022.

[206]Ibid., 1022-23.

gifts, that "the accuracy of any prophetic utterance will vary in proportion to the intensity of the gift and the faith of the one speaking".[207] Since the effect of a prophecy is linked to its quality, the power that it is announced with should be limited. This applies mainly at a super-structural level. We should not announce a prophecy from a person who does not have a proven record of prophetic ministry. However, it applies also to the personal level. Those who prophesy need to adjust the strength of their application/encouragement to match the clarity/conviction of the impression received.

Role

"Role" is Wimber's label for the ministry we are called to and equipped for due to our natural abilities. He calls it "the doing of the events which you see occurring in Scripture by means of your natural ability to the degree that you are able (rational)".[208] Grudem has a somewhat different model,[209] but thinks "there is some general ability similar to every gift that all Christians have".[210] His attempt to demonstrate this concerning tongues is questionable,[211] but it makes more sense concerning evangelism; "Not all Christians have a gift of evangelism, but all Christians have the ability to share the gospel with their neighbors." On the other hand, Wimber mentions "hospitality" as a *charisma* primarily based on the role of encouragement (1 Peter 4:9).[212]

To avoid giving people an excuse to be passive and to not serve because they do not have a particular gift for a ministry task which needs to be done is one of Wimber's concerns:

> This in essence is the working of the Spirit in giving gifts as He desires ... Everyone can and should render service, teach, exhort, give, etc. But at special times these activities will be anointed by God—

---

[207]Storms in Grudem, 1996, 209.

[208]Wimber, 1985b, 25.

[209]He suggests that "both Peter and Paul thought of gifts as abilities that were strong enough to function for the benefit of the church", Grudem, 1994, 1023.

[210]Grudem, 1994, 1023.

[211]He describes at ability that "gives expression to prayer in syllables that we do not fully understand [sighs, groans, weeping]", Grudem, 1994, 1024.

[212]Wimber, Anaheim 1983, 8.

gracelets.[213]

It must be noted that all the activities Wimber mentions as examples are so-called non-charismatic gifts. It is of course difficult to apply this point to the gift of prophecy for instance, but it is important to remember that Wimber does not make a distinction between supernatural and non-charismatic gifts. He lists these activities as charismatic events on the same level as prophecy (when commenting on Romans 12:6–8).[214]

Gracelets

"Gracelets/anointings" is Wimber's label on the first level of spiritual gifting. He defines it as,

> the occasional manifestations of a gift as ordained by God (transrational).[215]

The word "gracelets" was invented by Russell Spittler, a New Testament scholar at Fuller Theological Seminary. He defined them as "little manifestations of grace".[216] This is the "entry level" into gift-based ministry, and the level on which all the gifts are available to all believers. The punctual aspect of *charisma* is the basis of this understanding of spiritual gifts. I will explore the Biblical and grammatical basis for this label and concept in Chapter 7.

It seems like Wimber wants to put the focus on this entry level of ministry in spiritual gifts. From a pedagogical point of view this was understandable, since most people who listened to his teaching on the topic were not yet exercising spiritual gifts. He states: "Gifts are gracelets, anointings".[217] In the figure above the gracelet level is found at the lower left corner. The frequency and quality of the *charisma's* occurrence in the believer's life is occasional and variable.

Hunter quotes Spittler as having said, "the Spirit can manifest any of his gracelets through any of his people".[218] Spittler states—concerning gracelets—"I invented this little word," and then says that he allowed

---

[213]Wimber, 1985b, 25.
[214]Wimber 1985, 25-29.
[215]Wimber, 1985b, 25.
[216]Spittler, 1999.
[217]Wimber, 1985e.
[218] Hunter, 1999.

Wimber to pick it up and make it known.[219] He defines it as "little manifestations of grace." An interesting parallel is Vatican II's definition of charisms as "special graces by which he makes people able and willing to undertake various tasks or services".[220]

Wagner argues that what he calls "role" is similar to Wimber's "gracelets," but this must in my opinion be based on a misunderstanding,[221] because he describes role as what "every Christian is expected to do" and uses tithing as an example of a role, in comparison with the spiritual gift of giving.

It is particularly the *charismata* mentioned in Romans 12:6–8 that Wimber calls gracelets. Citing Dunn, he writes that gracelets, "with the exception of prophecy, are best seen as acts of service or ways of serving".[222]

> The gracelets are actions whose divine prompting is evidenced not by inspired speech or displays of power, but precisely by their character of service: that which serves the needs of fellow believers or the life of the community.[223]

Dunn writes, concerning charismatic authority: "the authority for proclamation, for evangelism, for healing, for individual word and action, for mission, was *presumably the authority of immediate inspiration and personal conviction, of vision*—in a word, *charismatic authority*".[224]

Storms writes about the gifts of healings and states, "When asked to pray for the sick, people are often heard to respond: 'I can't. I don't have the gift of healing'."[225] Wimber wrote that:

> Earlier when I read the gospels, I did not understand the admonishments to "do," "go," "speak," "heal the sick," etc. How? I asked. "I don't have the equipment." I did not know that you received the "how" when you started doing the "what".[226]

---

[219]Spittler, 1999.

[220]Vatican II, *Acta Synodalia*, 1963, 504.

[221]Wagner, 1994, 40.

[222]Dunn, 1975, 249.

[223]Wimber, 1985b, 25.

[224]Dunn, 1975, 178.

[225]Storms in Grudem, 1996, 212.

[226]Wimber, 1985c, 5.

Possession or Anointing

As I have already noted, Wimber's emphasis is on the gracelet/anointing level. In contrast to the traditional view, he writes that:

> There is a difference between the possession of gracelets and the gracelets being used by God through us at a special time and occasion. Many teachers of spiritual gifts have suggested that each person has a gift in his/her possession; they are dispensed to us and become our property. This does not appear to be the case. In 1 Corinthians we find that there are varieties (*diaireis*) or assignments of gracelets.[227]

Everybody can minister more or less frequently in all spiritual gifts in a limited dimension. The fact that a person has ministered in a particular gift several times does not necessarily mean that this person has to always minister in this gift—or always can. Even if a person is used by God to deliver a prophecy or to heal somebody on one or several occasions, that person does not automatically possess the respective gift. Wimber puts it like this:

> A believer does not possess gifts, a believer receives gifts from God to be used at special times for special occasions.[228]

A key to understand this principle is the fact that one never really receives a *charisma* to keep in one's possession, but to give away. Wimber bases his argument on 1 Corinthians 12:4–7, and points out concerning the source that "The same Spirit gives (sic.) the gracelets".[229] Concerning their use he states, "The root word here gives us our word 'deacon/servant.' Jesus is both the one ultimately served by the use of the gracelet and the one who directs to whom the service will be given." Concerning their effect, he argues that the root word here is *energematōn*, and that it is used here not in the active but in the completive sense; "God sees that the effects of the gracelets being used are accomplished."

Concerning their manifestation (*phanerōsis*), Wimber refers to Mel Robeck and writes that,

> The English word "manifestation" comes from two Latin words that

---

[227]Wimber, 1985c, 3.
[228]Ibid., 1.
[229]Ibid., 3.

means "the festive hand" or "the dancing hand." So the manifestations of the Spirit in verse 7 are the "dancing hand of God" which can be seen by all who observe. The word "given" in verse 7 is present tense, implying continuous action and could be translated "to each one he (God) is giving and keeps on giving. . ." The word is also passive. This means that "each one receives the giving from an outside source, i.e. the Spirit. This is not something which can be worked up" by oneself.[230]

It must be noted that Wimber's exegesis of the Latin basis for an English word should have been more clearly distinguished from the following exegesis of the Greek text. However, there are several supporting arguments for this somewhat untraditional position. First is it clear from 1 Corinthians 14:26b and the metaphor of the body in 1 Corinthians 12:14–27 that the *charismata* are given to the congregation for its edification. J. Rodman Williams suggests translating *diaireo* in 1 Corinthians 12:11 with "apportions." He thinks that all the *charismata* have both a divine and human side, but underlines that the gifts are

> primarily distributions of the Holy Spirit – the Spirit "apportions" or "distributes" – but the gifts operate in and through persons: He "apportions to each one" (1 Corinthians 12:11). In the operation of the spiritual gifts the Holy Spirit expresses himself in and through human activity.[231]

The word translated "apportions" is present tense, indicating continued activity over time. Grudem suggests therefore paraphrasing 1 Corinthians 12:11 like this:

> The Holy Spirit is always continuing to distribute or apportion gifts to each person individually just as he wills to do.[232]

Each healing is a gift which the sick person receives. Wimber does not state that this is a general principle that applies to all gifts, it does illustrate that he saw the one who received the benefit as the actual recipient of the gift.

"Anointings" is an alternative word[233] for gracelets, one which clearly

---

[230]Wimber, Section 4, 3.
[231]Williams, 1990, 332.
[232]Grudem, 1988, 1026.
[233]In Pentecostal and Faith-movement circles the word "anointing" carries a different

indicates that to minister in a spiritual gift on this level is a punctual, situational, and non-permanent equipping from God to do a specific service/task/ministry. In Chapter 10, I will look at the implications that this continuum from gracelets to ministry to gifted equipper (office) has for developing gifts. Gracelets, by their nature, are sovereignly given by God through us to others and therefore cannot be developed as a talent or skill, but they can be cultivated, leading to a "ministry". As Wimber wrote: "In time a gift evolves into ministry".[234] In Chapter 7, I will look more closely at the scriptural basis of this punctual and dynamic understanding of *charismata*.

Ministry

"Ministries" is Wimber's label on the middle level of spiritual gifting. He defines it as,

> The increase of occasions, use and dimensions of the gracelets.[235]

In Figure 2 ministry is found near the center. When the frequency of how often the *charisma* is expressed in the believer's life increases, and its quality or effect is dependable, it can be described as a ministry.

Wimber spoke of "prolonged anointings" and used healing as an example: "I noticed a few people who over a period of time were especially

---

meaning. The contrast with Wimber's view is illustrated by this quote from a Reinhart Bonnke sermon, where he emphasises anointing as a permanent possession:

> We got to learn to trust the anointing. I get disturbed to see that Christians all over the world is praying for a new anointing. What happened to the old one? Why do you think you need a new? I tell you why we think we need new anointings; It's because we confuse our emotions with the power of the Holy Spirit. Our feelings go up and down (like an elevator…basement…sky). Bonnke, 2001, 47.
>
> We think that the anointing moves like that. It is a mistake – the anointing doesn't move like that, our emotions move like that. . . . But when we talk about the anointing of the Holy Spirit, we speak about the eternal spirit of God. And there is another dimension to that. Ibid., 49.
>
> If you have been baptized in the Holy Ghost you have that anointing. Jesus says to you "I will never leave you' nor forsake you …I am with you always," and "the anointing which you have received of him abides with you" not coming or going . . . some people think that the anointing is like a nervous dove. The dove comes for five minutes, and then you make a harsh movement, and it's gone. Ibid., 50.

[234]Wimber, 1990, 154.
[235]Wimber, 1985c, 2.

effective in praying for the sick. They had a ministry of healing".[236] To put this in other words; when the frequency, dimension, and effect of the use of a particular *charisma* increases so the person is ministering in the *charisma* on a regular basis over a longer period of time, it can be said that the person has this "service" or "ministry." In everyday speech it can therefore be almost accurate to say that this person "has the gift" he or she is often ministering in. Wimber explained it like this:

> The gracelets plus ministry equals a job description. As God graces you with a gracelet and as he increases the frequency of such gracing in your life, ministry begins to take shape. You learn from each giving of the gracelet how better to work with God. The ministry which evolves becomes a job description.[237]

A crucial element in defining a person as having a ministry or gift is the trust that the person will be able to minister in the particular *charisma* if it should become necessary. For instance, a person can be allowed to share a message in tongues in a meeting even if there is nobody who has received the interpretation, as long as there is somebody present who has the ministry of interpreting tongues, based on a trust that this person will receive an interpretation today as well.

A ministry therefore consists of many gracelets, which create a stable continuum by their frequency. It is therefore a natural consequence that God at any time can "take away" a ministry, or more accurately, "stop giving" the particular type of gracelets to the person.

I will look more closely at the Biblical basis for these various "levels" of gifting below, as well as which gifts Paul mentions on each level.

Gifted equipper (office)

The top-level in Wimber's model is "gifted equipper (office)." This is what a ministry becomes when it has developed into maturity and effectiveness so that it becomes officially recognized by and somehow ordained by the church. Wimber defines gifted equipper (office) as,

> The appointments made by God, given to, and recognized by the church. God takes a person that he is using and gives her/him a

---

[236]Wimber, 1987, 206, quoted from Tangen, 1993, 27. See also Wimber, 1987, 141-142.
[237]Wimber, 1985c, 6.

functional gifted equipper (office).[238]

On the diagram above "gifted equipper (office)" is found at the top right corner, where both the frequency and the quality/effect is very high. Because Wimber emphasizes the functional aspect of gift-exercising over the personal aspect, Tangen labels Wimber's view of ecclesiastical gifted equippers (offices)[239] as "functional".[240] Turner affirmed that "some of the charismatic functions were simultaneously church 'gifted equippers (offices)' (at least of a rudimental type)".[241]

A central question regarding the development in Wimber's model from ministries to gifted equippers (offices) is whether manifestations constitute gifted equippers (offices), or if manifestations come after the initiation into gifted equippers (offices). Tangen addresses this question, and lists Luke 10:1ff, Acts 1:8, and 13:4 as examples of initiations into gifted equippers (offices) where the manifestations came after the initiation.[242] As examples of manifestations preceding the initiation into gifted equippers (offices) he lists Ananias (Acts 9:17–18), Stephen (Acts 6:8), and Philip (Acts 8:6f).[243] He lists also a few examples of manifestations without connections to gifted equippers (Acts 13:2, 19:6, and 21:9), but points out that it is possible that these manifestations could constitute gifted equippers (Acts 13:4 and 6:3).

Concerning the gifted equippers (offices) which have corresponding ministries, these are not so different from their respective ministries. The only major difference is the church's (the denomination or the local

---

[238]Ibid., 2.

[239]"*Embetssyn*".

[240]Tangen, 1993, 148. An interesting parallel to this view of gifted equippers (offices) can be found in Lutheran low-church circles in Norway. Hans Kvalbein defines this functional view as a "means of grace" focused view and adds that some variations of this view are particularly focused on the spiritual gifts. Eikli, 1991, 146-147. He writes that this view focuses on the fact that the mission of Christ to service with word and sacraments is given to the whole church, not only to a particular group.

[241]Turner, 1998, 282. He defines gifted equipper (office) as "a function (a) with an element of permanency, (b) recognized by the church (e.g. with a title), (c) authorized and allowed in some way, (d) with formal commissioning (e.g. through laying on of hands), and possibly (e) legitimated (through letter of commendation) and (f) remunerated". Ibid., 282.

[242]Tangen, 1993, 109.

[243]The last reference is questionable due to uncertainty connected to the laying on of hands in verse 5, but perhaps is it assumed that the Holy Spirit had been at work in their life earlier. Dunn, 1995, 177.

church) official recognition and ordination of the ministry. When it comes to the gifted equippers (offices) that do not directly correspond with particular ministries it is more complicated, since they more or less are based on a combination of different *charisma*. This is relevant when it concerns the gifted equipper (office) of apostle, but partly also when it concerns the gifted equippers (offices) of evangelist and pastor.[244]

In the context of the conflict with the Kansas Prophets, Wimber comments on the relationship between strong spiritual gifting, authority, and submission to the church. He argues against the presumption that a gift authenticates a person.

> I don't care if you're the finest communicator around, the finest expositor, the most brilliant theologue – if you can't come under the church . . . if you can't commit yourself to the leadership of others, if you can't commit yourself to collegiality and relationship, if you can't be inspected as well as teach, I don't want to play![245]

When commenting on the apostolic movement and current emphasis on the restoration of the "Five-Fold ministry," Wimber chooses to call these five gifted equippers (offices) "gifted equippers".[246]

> Ephesians 4:11–16 has been foundational for the ministry of the Vineyard since its inception. It lies at the very heart of our emphasis on equipping and releasing the Body to do the works of words of Jesus.

> The gifted equippers in Ephesians 4:11 are given by Christ to the church for the purpose of equipping the saints. These five designated areas of ministry are more *functions* that *persons* perform, and not any sort of gifted equippers (offices), although some commentators, in my opinion, are not careful in their use of terms (possibly because they are more thinkers than doers).

> In my opinion, though, neither the text nor the context of Ephesians 4:11–13 warrants us to assume that the gifted equippers must mean

---

[244]A general definition of "gifted equipper (office)" would have to take this into account, and could sound like this: "An gifted equipper (office) is a ministry recognized by the church consisting of one or several gifts or gracelets (*charisma*)."

[245]Packer in Pytches, 1998, 266.

[246] Wimber, 1997b.

gifted equippers (offices) which confer exceptional prerogatives, exclusive powers of grace, or structural authority over large portions (if not all) of the church.

> Paul is teaching that *equippers* are Christ's gift to the church, and these *equippers* are to function in the following ways through the gifts the risen Christ has given: [apostles, prophets, evangelists, pastors or pastor-teachers, teachers].[247]

Wimber underlines that "teacher," "pastor," "evangelist," "prophet," and "apostle" not are titles to bear or wear, but a stewardship to exercise in humility and love towards the whole church. Jesus loves the whole church, and so should we. The New Testament emphasizes function and serving the whole church, not claiming a gifted equipper (office) or calling oneself someone.[248]

THE *CHARISMATA* AS TOOLS

Wimber used "tools" as a metaphor for gracelets. This is perhaps the ultimate demonstration of the punctual nature of gracelets; totally independently of the person's normal ministry he/she can receive a "tool" from the Holy Spirit to use in a certain situation.

> Spiritual empowering equips one for service. The gifts are the tools which enable one to fulfill the ministry required.[249]

> They are not trophies, but tools. These are tools for touching and blessing others.[250]

Wimber's idea was that the Holy Spirit puts the tools that are needed for a specific ministry task in the believer's toolbox, and thereby equips the person to serve in a specific *charisma* in a specific situation. This toolbox metaphor must not be confused with the view that thinks all (the nine) gifts are residing in the believer's spirit because the Holy Spirit resides there, and thereby are readily available to the believer on his/her demand. Hunter refers to the "postman" as a related metaphor which emphasizes that it

---

[247]Wimber, 1997b, 11.
[248]Ibid., 10.
[249]Wimber, 1985c, 1.
[250]Wimber, 1991, 147.

depends on the giver (sender), not the gifts (letters). The emphasis in Wimber's theology is on the Holy Spirit's sovereignty in choosing whom he will work through when and how, not on the believers' right to exercise the gifts as if they owned and possessed them. I will come back to this in Chapter 6.

On the gracelet level, the use of various *charismata* is naturally limited to the Holy Spirit's genuine prompting. A more complex question which I cannot pursue here, is to what extent a believer with a more resident *charisma* and established ministry or gifted equipper (office) can make use of this *charisma* outside of God's will. Grudem calls the gifts "tools" as well, but he does not share Wimber's punctual understanding. He points out that the gifts are not related to maturity or a source of personal pride, but are "given for the work of ministry and are simply tools to be used for that end".[251] The main application of this metaphor is to encourage all believers to be open for irregular assignments.

SUMMARY

In this chapter I have presented Wimber's theology of *charismata* and focused on the notion of development from gracelet to ministry and to gifted equipper (office). He defined gifts/*charismata*/gracelets of the Holy Spirit as "transrational manifestations of God, bestowed upon us and through us", and believed that the arena where *charismata* should be exercised is in the marketplace, out on the streets, not in the church meetings.

The framework in which Wimber understood *charismata* was the Kingdom of God, which he described as "the invasion of God's rulership into the domain of Satan." He used "tools" as a metaphor for gracelets, picturing something enabling one to fulfill the ministry required. Even though he taught that believers did not possess gifts, but rather receives gifts from God to be used at special times for special occasions impartation, he balanced this by emphasizing that gifts are also imparted by the laying on of hands. He did not share the Pentecostal view on baptism in the Spirit as a post-conversion reception of the Holy Spirit marked with the gift of tongues, but rather as one of many "fillings."

"Role" is Wimber's label on the ministry we are called to and equipped

---

[251]Grudem, 1994, 1031.

for by means of our natural abilities. "Gracelets/anointings" he defines as "the occasional manifestations of a gift as ordained by God", and he puts the focus on this entry level of ministry in spiritual gifts. His basis for this is his punctual understanding of *charismata* as gift the believer does not possess, but receives from God to be used at special times for special occasions. Wimber's label on the middle level of spiritual gifting is "ministries", which he defined as "The increase of occasions, use and dimensions of the gracelets." The top level he calls "gifted equipper (office)," which he defines as "The appointments made by God, given to, and recognized by the church."

Wimber underlines that,

> all ministries, in my opinion, must be proven and released through the local church, confirmed in the field, give rise to the extension and expansion of churches, and be exercised with Christlike humility and love for the entire Body of Christ.[252]

---

[252]Wimber, 1997b, 10.

2: IMPLICATIONS OF THE DYNAMIC VIEW

For the Characteristics and Functions of some Charismata

In this chapter I will look more closely at a few *charismata* and analyze what implications Wimber's dynamic aspects have for the definitions, characteristics, and functions, of these gifts.

CATEGORIZATION OF THE *CHARISMATA*

Wimber categorized the *charismata* into three groups:[253]

1. The Gracelets of *Discernment*: The Eyes of God.

2. The Gracelets of *Power*: The Hand of God.

3. The Gracelets of *Speech*: The Mouth of God.

Wimber acknowledges that this "was probably not Paul's intention, [but] it is useful as a teaching tool".[254] Since Wimber's teaching on *charismata* was organized as expository teaching going through each single passage, he did not include the gracelets that did not appear in 1 Corinthians 12 in

---

[253]An alternative way to categorize the gifts is to use the Old Testament gifted equippers (offices) and distinguish between "priestly," "kingly," and "prophetic" gifts (Grudem, 1996, 1021). Other alternatives are to separate between "gifts of revelation," "gifts of power," and "inspirational or fellowship gifts" (Bennett, 1971, 83), or between "love gifts," "power gifts," and "word gifts" (Clinton and Clinton, 1998,126). A simplistic way to sort the gifts is to use the two categories in 1 Peter 4:11; "those who speak," and "those who render service." To distinguish between "natural" and "supernatural" gifts has stronger theological implications, but I have chosen not to enter this debate since Wimber nowhere makes this distinction. See Grudem, 1994, 1027.

[254]Wimber, 1985b, 1.

the above-mentioned system. He described a group of the gracelets in Romans as "acts of service or ways of serving." This category could therefore be called "The Gracelets of Service; The Heart of God." The gracelets in Ephesians Wimber listed separately.

A question most theologians who write about spiritual gifts treat at length is "how many spiritual gifts exist?" Since Wimber's view is shared with most students of *charismata*, including myself, holding that the number of *charismata* is open, I will only briefly mention some potential *charismata*. Spittler comments that he is missing "exorcism (Paul has very little to say about demons), counseling, preacher, eunuch, [and] hospitality in Paul's lists".[255] Bugbee adds "creative communication," and writes, "some would affirm: celibacy, counseling, deliverance, martyrdom and voluntary poverty as gifts",[256] and Grudem adds "marriage" (1 Corinthians 7:7).

F3: Categorization of the Charismata *(Adapted from Wimber 1985)*		
Category	Charisma	Scripture
Gracelets of Discernment: the Eyes of God	Word of knowledge	1 Corinthians 12:8
	Word of wisdom	1 Corinthians 12:8
	Discernings of spirits	1 Corinthians 12:10
The Gracelets of Power: The Hand of God	Faith	1 Corinthians 12:9
	Gifts of healings	1 Corinthians 12:9
	Effects of Miracles/Powers	1 Corinthians 12:10
The Gracelets of Speech: The Mouth of God	Prophecy	1 Corinthians 12:10
	Kinds of tongues	1 Corinthians 12:10
	Interpretation of tongues	1 Corinthians 12:10
	Apostleship[257]	1 Corinthians 12:28
	Teaching	Romans 12:7
	Ruling/leadership/administration	Romans 12:8
	Exhortation	1 Corinthians 12:28
Other gracelets The Gracelets of Service:	Service	Romans 12:7
	Giving, Aid, Mercy	1 Corinthians 12:8

---

[255]Spittler, 1999.

[256]Bugbee et. al., 1994, 9.

[257]Wimber did not include this gracelet in this category since his overview was limited it to the gracelets mentioned in 1 Corinthians 12. He mainly deals with these gracelets as gifted equippers (offices) based on Ephesians 4:11.

The Heart of God		1 Corinthians 12:28
The Gracelets of Ephesians	Apostle	Ephesians 4:11
	Pastor-teacher	Ephesians 4:11
	Prophet	Ephesians 4:11 1 Corinthians 12:28
	Evangelist	Ephesians 4:11
Possible gracelets listed in various passages	Celibacy	1 Corinthians 7:7
	Craftsmanship	Exodus 31:3, 25:31–33
	Hospitality	1 Peter 4:9
	Interpretation of Dreams	Genesis 41:25–32, 38–39
	Judge	Jud.3:7–11
	Philanthropy	1 Corinthians 13:3
Other possibilities	Intercessory Prayer	
	Missionary Cross cultural Ministry	
	Music	Psalm 150:3–5
	Worship Leader	1 Corinthians 14:26

It hardly needs to be pointed out that Wimber's attempt to organize the gifts into the categories "discernment" "power" and "speech," does not account for all of the gifts, as this had clearly not been his intention, but rather as a grouping of the *charismata* in 1 Corinthians 12.

DESCRIPTIONS OF SOME *CHARISMATA*

I will now look at each of these categories and focus on some of the *charismata* which are affected by Wimber's dynamic aspects from each category. The main purpose of this section is to study the implications which this dynamic view has for each particular gift. The presentation is mainly based on Wimber's own definitions and comments about each gift.

Gracelets of Discernment

Wimber describes the function of the gracelets of discernment as "The Eyes of God," which Hunter explains as indicating "God's perspective." Wimber includes the following gifts in this category; "word of knowledge," "word of wisdom," and "discernings of spirits." I will only go into detail about the first two. He defines the category like this:

> The gracelets of Discernment—Word of Wisdom, Word of Knowledge, and Discernings of spirits, are gifts of supernatural insight. They see things as God sees them. Speech is required in order to communicate these discernments. These gracelets meet the Christian's need for having God's insight into their circumstances. They are not perceptions from a rational base. A person cannot think them up on his own or communicate them on his own. They are transrational.[258]

In the framework of the battle metaphor, Wimber describes the purpose of discernment of spirits as "to discover the real enemy behind the camouflage".[259]

Word of Knowledge - logos gnōseōs

Wimber defines the *charisma* of "word of knowledge"[260] like this:

> A word of Knowledge is an utterance inspired by God and spoken by an individual. It is an insight into the things freely given us by God (1 Corinthians 2:12). It shares the truth of facts which the Spirit wishes declared concerning a specific occasion with a practical application of an outpouring of God's love.[261]

Wimber believed that we can expect a *logos gnōseōs* "in situations where God's insight is needed," and that it can come in one of five ways: "Pictures, inner knowing, a picture of a written word, pain in the body, a spontaneous utterance which comes without your volition".[262] He summarizes it like this; "you 'see' it, 'know' it, 'read' it, 'feel' it, 'say' it," and divides the arenas of use for this *charisma* into five categories:

1. To reveal sin (2 Samuel 21:1–7, 2 Kings 5:20–27, John 4:7–25, Acts 5:1–6),

---

[258]Wimber, 1985b, 1-2.

[259]Ibid., 6.

[260]See also 1 Corinthians 2:14; 1 Corinthians 12:8; Acts 5:1-11; Colossians 2:2-3; 2 Corinthians 11:6.

[261]Ibid., 4.

[262]Ibid., 5.

2. To help find something (1 Samuel 9:15, 1 Samuel 10:22),

3. To warn and provide safety (2 Kings 6:8–23),

4. To reveal thoughts (Matthew 9:1–7), and

5. To provide healing (Matthew 9:1–7, John 4:45–54, John 5:1–9).[263]

The *Network Manual* from Willow Creek Community Church presents the gift as a kind of intellectual capacity:

> KNOWLEDGE—The gift of knowledge is the special ability that God gives to certain members of the body of Christ to discover, accumulate, analyze, and clarify information and ideas which are pertinent to the growth and wellbeing of the body.[264]

A similar view is defended by Grudem, who understands word of knowledge as "the ability to speak with knowledge about a situation," and word of wisdom as "the ability to speak a wise word in various situations".[265] He does not understand it as spontaneous revelation, but as "the knowledge and wisdom that would be characteristic of Bible teachers and elders and other mature Christians in a church, for example." He bases this view on three main arguments:

1. *Sophia* and *logos* "are not specialized or technical terms but are extremely common words … [and] not ordinarily used to miraculous events".[266]

2. Paul's purpose "is to demonstrate that no matter what kind of gift a person has, he or she can be assured that the gift is given by the Holy Spirit".[267] Since all the other gifts in 1 Corinthians 12:8–10 are miraculous gifts, these two must be examples of non-miraculous gifts.

---

[263]Ibid., 5.
[264]Bugbee et. al., 1994, 33.
[265]Grudem, 1994, 1080.
[266]Ibid., 1081.
[267]Ibid., 1081.

3. The term "prophecy" describes "the action of receiving a special revelation from the Holy Spirit and reporting it in the congregation".[268]

While Grudem's view, like Bugbee's, is that it is not spontaneous, he does clearly include the situational aspect as did Wimber.

Fee translates it "message (logos) of knowledge (*gnōsis*)" and thinks that it "most likely . . . is a 'spiritual utterance' of some revelatory kind".[269] He says the phenomenon is described in 1 Corinthians 14:24–25, Mark 2:8, John 1:48, 4:16ff, Acts 8:23.[270] Peter's knowledge of Ananias and Sapphira's misdeed in Acts 5:1–11 is often looked upon as this gift in action.[271] The phenomenon is most likely closely associated to clairvoyance. In the Old Testament, the prophets were often called "seers" 1 Samuel 9:9, Jeremiah 30:30.[272]

Brent Rue lists Matthew 9:2, John 4:50, and John 5:6 as examples of connections between word of knowledge and sickness.[273] Tangen adds John 9:3 and thinks that *ginōskō* is used with revelatory character in John 17:3, 14:17, etc.

As Wimber understood and defined this gift, it was the perfect "beginner's tool" to be used spontaneously by all Christians. Uttering simple pieces of knowledge about diseases or situations provides for an often-needed "beginner-type" of prophecy. Nevertheless, I must agree with those who argue that "word of knowledge" is not an accurate term for the phenomena Wimber describes.

Dunn argues that "word of wisdom" is virtually synonymous with "word of knowledge," and

> may be thought of as some kind of practical, even earthly advice, though presumably inspired advice arising out of recognition of God's *Heilsplan* and *Heilsgut*.[274]

Tangen suggests calling it "prophetic insight or revelation",[275] and Stanley

---

[268]Ibid., 1082.
[269]Fee, 1987, 592-3.
[270]Tangen, 1993, 117.
[271]Fee, 1987, 593.
[272]Tangen, 1993, 117.
[273]Brent Rue, 1988, 13.
[274]Dunn 1975, 221.
[275]Tangen, 1993, 117.

Horton puts it very clearly:

> God did give knowledge of facts through visions and in various
> other ways, but there is absolutely no indication in the Bible that the
> gift of a word of knowledge is meant to bring revelation of where to
> find lost articles or of what disease or sin a person may be suffering
> with.[276]

The Scripture does not provide much material to build a comprehensive
understanding of this *charisma*, but I believe this definition by Williams
might point in a direction that makes sense. He views *logos gnōseōs* as "essentially an inspired word of teaching or instruction that occurs within the
context of the gathered community",[277] and his interpretation of *logos
gnōseōs* is connected to his understanding of *logos sophias* (see below). He
thinks that *logos gnōseōs*, like *logos sophias*,

> is concerned about the truth of God but operates more in terms of
> articulation. It is the knowledge of a spiritually enlightened mind
> that, in correspondence therewith, clearly sets forth the truth for
> others to understand. It is utterance stemming from an inspired
> knowledge . . . Word of knowledge makes the things of God under-
> standable to His people.[278]

It is outside the scope of this chapter to arrive at a definition of this gift,
but I will conclude that the case against Wimber's definition must be regarded as strong. I do not question the practice of receiving and giving
"words of knowledge," but I do not see any strong reasons why this type of
prophecy should have its own label (and thereby occupy this Biblical label),
since various types of prophetic messages (like dreams, visions, pictures,
prophetic songs, etc.) all are included in the prophecy-label. Since we find
this gift mentioned only once by Paul it would be best to not focus strongly
on it. Nevertheless, I do not find the widespread use of the label "word of
knowledge" with Wimber's definition harmful, since the practice of this
gift can be regarded as a kind of prophecy.

---

[276]Horton. 1979. 272-73.

[277]Williams, 1990, 356.

[278]Ibid., 357.

Word of Wisdom - *logos sophias*

Wimber defines the *charisma* of "word of wisdom"[279] like this:

> A Word of Wisdom is an utterance inspired by God and spoken by an individual. It reveals a part of the total wisdom of God. It is seeing what God sees in a situation and saying it. It is applying God's wisdom to a specific situation.[280]

Wimber believes that a *logos sophias* can be expected in "any situation which requires problem solving, in counseling, [and] in the proclamation of the Word".[281] He describes the way it comes in the following:

- You will see in a revelatory way what is being said or done from God's perspective. It will sometimes be a mind's eye picture. Sometimes it comes with a Word of Knowledge with facts which you did not know before.

- Sometimes an utterance of wisdom comes as a prophetic utterance and has all the characteristics of prophecy.

- Word of Wisdom almost always comes in the exchange that is happening at the time.[282]

Wimber uses three stories of problems that were solved by *logos sophias* as illustrations of this *charisma* in use.

- Solomon's command to "divide the child in two" revealed who was the real mother (1 Kings 3:16–28).

- Jesus' question of whose likeness the coin carried left the Pharisees marveling (Matthew 22:15–22).

- James' decision concerning the circumcision of the Gentiles created an agreement (Acts 15:5–27).

Wimber also points to Genesis 41:14–15, 2 Kings 5:8–14, Matthew 21:23–27, and John 7:53–8:11 as illustrations.

For the purpose of comparison, I have included Costa Mitchell's definition:

---

[279]See 1 Corinthians 2:1-13; 1 Corinthians 12:8; Acts 6:3,10; James.1:5,6; 2 Peter 3:15-16.
[280]Wimber, 1985b. 2.
[281]Ibid., 2.
[282]Ibid., 3.

> WISDOM—The gift of wisdom is the special ability that God gives to certain members of the body of Christ to know the mind of the Holy Spirit in such a way as to receive insight into how given knowledge may best be applied to specific needs arising in the body of Christ.[283]

While Wimber describes this *charisma* as a kind of prophetic utterance, Mitchell is describing it as an ability to apply knowledge. It is not clear if he means Biblical knowledge or factual knowledge or knowledge derived from "words of knowledge," but his definition shares, at least the possibility for, this *logos sophias* to be punctual and not necessarily permanent.

Williams believes that it is crucial to link *logos sophias* to its antidote, "human wisdom," which Paul did not preach (1 Corinthians 1:17), and to the twenty-five times "wisdom/wise/wiser" is mentioned in chapter 1–3. Based on this he defines *logos sophias* as,

> in some way an explanation of the mystery of God that centers in Jesus Christ . . . that which speaks of Christ, particularly the cross, is an utterance or word of wisdom.[284]

Williams underlines that "a word of wisdom does not depend on one's being a wise person or persuasive preacher" but states that "preaching, or proclamation, that sets forth Christ under the anointing of the Spirit is the utterance of spiritual wisdom".[285] Dunn argues along the same line, and explains the background: "*Gnōsis* and *sophia* are the slogans of the faction [who claimed to alone possess these] opposing Paul in Corinth".[286] He thinks that Paul redefines these words, writing, "for Paul wisdom and knowledge are not to be taught of as *charismata*; only the actual utterance which reveals wisdom or knowledge to others is a *charisma*".[287]

Spittler translates logos here as "the capacity to reason, intelligence, the act of reasoning, cognition, outcome/product of thinking (written or oral), the study of this," and suggests that Paul's use of this phrase "may be throwaway usage; an instance of wisdom, or occasion of wisdom".[288] He

---

[283]Mitchell, 1999, 33.

[284]Williams, 1990, 350.

[285]Ibid., 353.

[286]Dunn, 1995, 217.

[287]Ibid., 221.

[288]Splitter, 1999.

describes the classic Pentecostal interpretation as "declaration of secret," which is very close to Wimber's view, and thinks that the "text allows it, but doesn't demand it".[289]

A dynamic view is a necessary basis for Wimber's definition, which is more punctual than William and Spittler's definitions. Since this *charisma* is only named once in Scripture, I have chosen to avoid drawing conclusions about it. Like *logos gnōseōs*, Wimber's definition comes close to prophecy.

Gracelets of Power

Wimber describes the function of the group of *charismata* he calls the "Gracelets of Power," as "The Hand of God," and includes the following gifts in this category—faith, gifts of healings, and effects of miracles. I will limit this presentation to the first two. He defines the category like this:

> . . . the Gracelets of Power have to do with the power of God, Faith, Gifts of Healing, and Effects or Miracles (or Works of Power) are the gracelets in which the supernatural power of God is seen. These gracelets are the acts of God, the divine energy of God which accomplishes a particular result in word or work through an individual. There is often an interrelationship between these three gracelets.[290]

Gifts of Healings – Charismata Iamatōn

Wimber defines the "gifts of healings" like this:

> The gifts of healings are the actual event of healing itself which a sick person receives. As there are many kinds of illnesses, so there are many different healing gifts. It is that event or progression which a person receives in the emotional, spiritual, or physical areas of life.[291]

In the framework of the battle metaphor Wimber describes the purpose of healing as "to defeat the enemy, bring to wholeness those who have been wounded in the battle".[292]

Wimber sees divine healing as an effect of the atonement, not a part of

---

[289]Ibid.
[290]Wimber, 1985b, 8.
[291]Ibid., 9.
[292]Ibid., 6.

it,[293] and views it as a natural part of the service of the church due to the fact that "the kingdom of God is near" (Mark 1:14). He holds a theocentric view of the kingdom of God and defines healing as the "manifestation of the Kingdom of God".[294]

This is clearly one of the gifts for which a dynamic view has the strongest implications. Healing is a central part of "signs and wonders." It was Wimber's passion to equip all believers to minister in healing.

Grudem points out that the purpose of healing is fourfold. It is "a 'sign' to authenticate the gospel message, and show that the kingdom of God has come".[295] Further, it "brings comfort and health to those who are ill," it "equips people for service," and it "provides opportunity for God to be glorified."

The double plural in *charismata iamatōn* can be understood in at least four ways:

1. There is one *charisma* for each disease.

2. Each occurrence of healing is a distinct *charisma*.

3. The actual healing somebody receives is the *charisma*.

4. There is one healing *charisma*.

C. Samuel Storms argues that 1 or 2 above is the correct interpretation, because:

> Both words are plural and lack the definite article in Greek (*charismata iamatōn*). Evidently, Paul did not envision that a person would be endowed with one healing gift, operative at all times, for all diseases [4]. His language suggests either many differing gifts or powers of healing, each appropriate to and effective for its related illness [1], or each occurrence of healing constituting a distinct gift in its own right [2].[296]

Williams argues that 3 is correct, based on the fact that Paul earlier (verse 4) used *charismata* to refer to "varieties of gifts," that "hence the gift is not healings as such but gifts or *charismata* of healings".[297] He explains that the

---

[293]Wimber, 1988, 192.

[294]Tangen, 1993, 13.

[295]Grudem, 1994, 1064.

[296]Storms in Grudem, 1996, 212.

[297]Williams, 1990, 367.

one who receives such gifts does not directly perform the healings, rather he simply transmits the gifts. He is a kind of "delivery boy" who brings the gifts to others. Hence such a person does not become a healer even for a moment, he or she simply passes on the healings to others.[298]

Fee shares Storms' view, and comments that "the plural *charismata* probably suggests not a permanent 'gift' [4] as it were, but that each occurrence is a 'gift' in its own right" [2].[299] Bittlinger makes a similar suggestion, writing, "every healing is a special gift [2 or 3]—in this way the spiritually gifted individual stands always in new dependence upon the divine giver".[300]

The first option above [1] also deserves some consideration. I have not discovered any attempts by Wimber to theologize on this, but it is acknowledged in the Vineyard movement that some people can be especially effective in praying for certain diseases, like for instance uneven legs, which was Peter Wagner's "specialty".[301] I doubt that this is an adequate definition of *charismata iamatōn*, but it highlights an important aspect, namely, "even as there are many sicknesses and diseases, the gifts relate to healings or cures for many disorders".[302]

As shown in Wimber's definition of *charismata iamatōn* above, he is teaching that option 2 is the correct one, but he sees option 2 as a premise for this, stating that, as "there are many kinds[303] of illnesses so there are many healing gracelets." In Chapter 7 I will ask whether there is anything like an gifted equipper (office) of "healer." A dynamic and punctual understanding of *charismata* is a necessary basis for this view on gifts of healing as separate healings.

Faith

Wimber defines the *charisma* of "faith" like this:

> Faith is the mysterious urge of confidence which sometimes arises within a person faced with a specific situation or need. It gives that

---

[298]Ibid., 367.

[299]Fee, 1987, 594.

[300]Bittlinger, 1967, 37. See Chapter 2 concerning the recipients of gifts of healing.

[301]Wagner in Springer, editor, 1987, 8.

[302]Williams, 1990, 366.

[303]"Kinds of diseases" is here most likely referring to individual diseases, not to types of diseases.

person a transrational (otherly) certainty and assurance that God is about to act through a word or action.[304] It is both the irresistible knowledge of God's intervention at a certain point and their authority to effect this intervention through the power of the Holy Spirit.[305]

The punctual nature of this *charisma* hardly needs to be argued. Wimber emphasizes that this is a special gift given for a purpose, like in Mark 2 . Commenting on the Centurion's faith in Luke 7, he writes:

> The size of the faith doesn't matter, but where you place that faith. Not in yourself, or on past experiences, or the Vineyard or etc. The only thing which matters is to depend on God.[306]

Wimber taught that faith was one of the most important gifts in healing situations, but unlike much teaching on healing, he did not believe that the success of the healing prayer depended on the faith of the person who asked for prayer. "Someone must always have faith if a healing shall occur (it doesn't need to be the prayor or prayee, it can be a third person (often child)".[307] He describes three types of faith:

F4: *Types of Faith* (Adapted from Wimber)[308]		
Type	**Example**	**Description**
The faith command	Acts 3:1–10	Peter and John at the Gate called Beautiful
Faith pronouncement	2 Kings 4	Elijah tells the woman to find many empty jars
Faith expulsion	Acts 16	Some tough demons are hard to get out

Hunter refers to Williams' book *Renewal Theology* as a recommendable resource on our subject. Williams calls *pistis* "special faith",[309] and describes it as,

> the first of a series of gifts that operate in distinction from the mind. These gifts—faith, healing, effects of miracles, prophecy, and distinguishing of spirits—are particular active ministry gifts. They

---

[304]Wimber citing Dunn, 1975, 211.
[305]Wimber, 1985b, 8.
[306]Ibid, 8.
[307]Wimber, 1985d.
[308]Ibid.
[309]Williams, 1990, 358.

represent a faith flowing out in action.[310]

He also suggests that faith

> may be the immediate background for the exercise of the two ministry gifts that follow: the gifts of healings, and the effecting of miracles. Faith is the atmosphere in which healing occurs; it is likewise the basic precondition for the working of.[311]

Based on this understanding of the punctual role the *charisma* of faith plays in relation to healing and miracles, a dynamic model is almost a prerequisite!

Gracelets of Speech

Wimber describes the function of the "Gracelets of Speech" as "The Mouth of God," and includes the following gifts in this category—"prophecy," "kinds of tongues, "interpretation of tongues." I will suggest adding "exhortation," "apostleship," "teaching" and "administration (ruling/leadership)" to this category since Wimber has either not included these *charismata* in any category, or only treated them as gifted equippers (offices) based on Ephesians 4:11. I believe this might be in line with Wimber because he limited his categories to 1 Corinthians 12.

Wimber shows that he views "teaching" as a leadership gift when he describes the purpose of teaching as "to give instructions on how to wage the war" in his battle metaphor.[312] "Exhortation" he links to prophecy, and "administration" he defines as leadership/ruling (see definition below). He does not define this category, but states that "These [gracelets] are provided by God for the purpose of communication".[313]

I will now look closer at prophecy, tongues/interpretation, and administration.

Prophecy[314]

Wimber uses Dunn's definition of the *charisma* of "prophecy":

---

[310]Ibid., 358.

[311]Ibid., 359.

[312]Wimber, 1985b, 6.

[313]Ibid., 12.

[314]Clinton and Clinton, 1998, 308 provides a careful exegesis on the nature and function of

> Prophecy is declaring the heartthrob of God to His Church for the purpose of edification. It is not a skill or aptitude or talent. It is the actual speaking forth of words given by the Spirit in a particular situation and ceases when the Word ceases.[315]

Prophecy is the only consistent *charisma* in all of Paul's lists,[316] and the New Testament contains so many accounts of its use in the early church that it should be possible to build our understanding of it on those examples. Even so, many non-charismatics, especially cessationists, believe prophecy must be understood as preaching. Clinton argues from the fact that Paul instructed the one prophesying to prophesy "in proportion to his faith" (Romans 12:6), that it "doesn't make sense to translate [*propheteian* with] preaching".[317]

Wimber makes an important distinction between the authoritative prophecies in the Old Testament and contemporary prophecy:

> Our contemporary prophecies are not to be accorded the same status as Scripture. Today's prophecies—at what could be called the "popular level of prophecy"—are God's repeated messages of strengthening, encouragement, and comfort. They can be prefaced by "Now hear this". They are for the moment. I teach that prophecy today should not be written down and collected; such collections can distract people from the Bible and lead them into heresies.[318]

In the framework of the battle metaphor, Wimber says the purpose of prophecy is "to give us encouragement in and direction for the battle".[319] It must be noted that Wimber, for a period, was strongly influenced by the Kansas City prophets and allowed a strong focus on prophets and prophetic messages, but later regretted having let the prophets exercise leadership over the church.

Wimber distinguishes between Old Testament and New Testament

---

the gift of prophecy today: "While holding to the sufficiency of Scripture to every aspect of our lives, . . . [He] sees the blessing and the importance of exercising the gift of prophecy in churches today". Also Wayne Grudem, *The Gift of Prophecy in the New Testament and Today*, 1988.

[315]Ibid., 12, citing Dunn, 1975, 229.

[316]See Chapter 7.

[317]Clinton, 1999.

[318]Wimber, 1991, 158.

[319]Wimber, 1985b, 6.

prophetic ministry:

> OT prophets were sent by God (Haggai 1:13, Obadiah.1:1) and spoke and wrote words which had absolute divine authority (2 Peter 1:19–21, Numbers 22:38, Exodus 7:1, Jeremiah 1:19)…OT prophetic ministry ceased with the last and greatest prophets of the OT prophets, John the Baptist (Luke 1:76, Matthew 11:9–13), and most of these ministry functions were passed on to the Apostles, not to the NT prophets.[320]

> NT prophets spoke words which God had laid on their hearts for strengthening, encouraging, and comforting the Body (1 Corinthians 14:30). Their words were never prefaced with "thus says the Lord," and did not always come to pass (Acts 21:11, "Jews would bind Paul,"22:29 "Romans put Paul in chains"). The recipients of prophecy, therefore, needed to test, weigh, interpret and then apply what was good (Paul and his journey to Jerusalem, Acts 20:23, 21:4–13, also 1 Corinthians 14:29, 1 Thessalonians 5:19–22, Acts.11:27). NT prophets operated under the church government (1 Corinthians 14:29–31)".[321]

A theologian, who was strongly influenced by Wimber, and can be regarded as representative of the Wimber's view, is Wayne Grudem. He argues that the correct definition of the gift of prophecy, is "telling something that God has spontaneously brought to mind," not as "predicting the future" or "proclaiming a word from the Lord".[322] His basis for this is a comparison with the Old Testament prophets, who had an "amazing responsibility: they were able to speak and write words that had absolute divine authority".[323] He is surprised to find that their counterparts in the New Testament are called "apostles," and states, "it is the apostles, not the prophets, who have authority to write the very words of the New Testament Scripture."[324] He thinks this transition was due to the contemporary meaning of

---

[320]Wimber, 1997b, 12.

[321]Ibid., 12.

[322]Grudem, 1994, 1049.

[323]Ibid., 1050.

[324]See 1 Corinthians 2:13, 2 Corinthians 13:3, Galatians 1:8-9, 11-12, 1 Timothy 2:13, 4:8, 15, 2 Peter 3:2.

> the Greek word *prophetes*. . . as "one who speaks on the basis of some external influence"[325] (often a spiritual influence of some kind) . . . not as "one who speaks God's very words".[326]

The basis for Grudem's definition is a broad interpretation of "revelation" as "something that God may suddenly bring to mind, or something that God may impress on someone's consciousness in such a way that the person has a sense that it is from God".[327] He therefore concludes: "Prophecy occurs when a revelation from God is reported in the prophet's own (merely human) words",[328] and underlines the edifying content it should have, based on 1 Corinthians 14:3: "He who prophesies speaks to men for their upbuilding and encouragement and consolation".

A key implication of a dynamic view of the *charisma* of prophecy is the theological basis it provides for encouraging all believers to ask and listen to God for encouraging words to share with people around them. Many people who have attended a Vineyard conference or service and have experienced a typical "ministry time" might have been encouraged to turn toward their neighbor in order to pray together and ask God for words for each other.

Kinds of Tongues and Interpretation of Tongues

Wimber defines the *charismata* of "kinds of tongues" and "interpretation of tongues" like this:

> Tongues is Spirit-inspired speaking in which the conscious mind plays no part. It is the speaking of a language (whether known or angelic) which is unlearned by the speaker.

Grudem points to the fact that "the Greek word *glōssa*, translated 'tongue,' is used not only to mean the physical tongue in a person's mouth, but also to mean 'language'".[329] He argues therefore that the correct translation is "speaking in languages," and sees it as "something of a foretaste of the unity of language that will exist in heaven".[330] He thinks that tongues is

---

[325]See Titus 1:12, Luke 22:64, John 4:19.
[326]Ibid., 1050.
[327]Ibid., 1056.
[328]Ibid., 1057.
[329]Gruden, 1994, 1069.
[330]Ibid., 1070.

"primarily speech directed toward God" and defines it along the same lines as Wimber, writing: "Speaking in tongues is prayer or praise spoken in syllables not understood by the speaker".[331]

"Glossalia" is not a biblical word. It was made up in the 18th century from two Greek words, *glōssa* and *laleō*. [332]

> Human glossalia can be viewed on a continuum from groaning, to simple language forms, to language forms, to known language. Any of this might come as a result of the Spirit, but also without—it can be generated by human will.[333]

Concerning interpretation of tongues, Wimber writes that,

> The Interpretation of Tongues is the God-given inspiration to speak in the language of the listeners, giving them the dynamic equivalent of that which was spoken in tongues.[334]

Howard Carter explains that the interpreter "will be in the Spirit at the time when the utterance in tongues is given, so that the words will be registered on his spirit and he will feel the urge to speak what God gives him".[335] T. B. Barrat distinguishes between four types of interpretation:

1. After a person has finished speaking with tongues, the meaning of the spoken words is comprehensively interpreted, but it is not translated word by word.

2. The interpretation may be just an outline of the glossalia message.

3. It may be given little by little and sentence by sentence, or

4. "word by word".[336]

Based on the command in 1 Corinthians 14:28 to "Keep silent if there is no interpreter present" Spittler comments that this "must mean that it is possible to know if there is an interpreter present".[337]

Spittler says, "different kinds (genus) of" is a classification term. The

---

[331]Ibid., 1069-70.
[332]Spittler, 1999.
[333]Ibid.
[334]Wimber, 1985b, 14.
[335]Literal translation, cited in Bloch-Hoell, 1972, 145.
[336]Ibid., 145.
[337]Spittler, 1999.

meaning of this phrase is therefore "categories or types of tongues".[338] The following table presents possible "kinds of" tongues.

F5: Different Kinds of Tongues			
Kind of tongues	Directed to	Interpretation	Public/private use
praise/worship	God	no interpretation	both
thanksgiving	God	can be interpretation	both
prophetic	congregation	must be interpretation	public
preaching	congregation	intelligible language	public
prayer	God	no interpretation	private

On a technical level glossalia can be grouped into four types:

1. "Inarticulate sounds or utterings,

2. Articulate sounds or pseudo-language,

3. Articulate and combined, language-like sounds, art or fantasy language,

4. Automated speech in a real language, either a native language or xenolalia".[339]

It is not likely that any of these is the "kinds of tongues" Paul is referring to.

A dynamic view of the *charisma* of tongues is incompatible with a Pentecostal view of prayer-tongues as the mandatory sign of reception of or baptism in the Spirit.[340] Nevertheless, the acceptance of a dynamic view by a person with a Pentecostal theology who had "lost" his prayer-tongue, and thereby feared that he had lost the Holy Spirit, would be of great comfort.

Administration (Governments/Ruling/Leadership)

Wimber points out that the modern phenomenon of administrative structures and institutions has thinned our understanding of Scripture. He cites Dunn, who suggests that perhaps we should strive for nothing more

---

[338]Ibid.

[339]Bloch-Hoell, 1972, 143.

[340]For further presentation of the Pentecostal doctrine of the Holy Spirit, see "The Pentecostal View" in Chapter 6.

precise that "giving guidance".[341]

I have chosen to translate *kybernesis* as "administration" throughout this thesis, but it is possible that a more accurate translation is "giving counsel"[342] or "acts of guidance".[343] Fee admits that "the cognate personal noun for this word occurs in Acts 27:11 and Revelation 18:17, meaning 'steersman' or 'pilot'". Based on its use as guidance in Proverbs 1:5, 11:14, and 24:6, he believes it is "likely that it refers to giving wise counsel to the community as a whole, not only to individuals".[344] Based on Dunn, Wimber defines the gift of administration as "the gracelet provided by God for giving direction or guidance to the Body of Christ",[345] and as

> getting insight and direction from God, and being able to communicate that to the body in such ways that it would result in the steering, directing, governing of the local body, and/or maybe also a larger group if it is denominational or broader church.[346]

Wimber says that as a pastor or helmsman for a church, he is "to look for these administrating gracelets, where God will say; this is the emphasis, and this is the focus for the church at this time". Clearly, the way he defines this gift is similar to the way Clinton and Clinton defines "ruling/leadership":

> A person operating with a ruling gift demonstrates the capacity to exercise influence over a group so as to lead it toward a goal or purpose with a particular emphasis on the capacity to make decisions and keep the group operating together.[347]

The definition above is based on the translation of *proistamenos* in Romans 12:8 as leadership/ruling. Wimber, on the other hand, translated this as "aid" since it is placed between two forms of aid/giving, and he defined it as "caring for others." In line with this, he argues that 1 Thessalonians 5:12 should be translated: "Who diligently labor among you and give aid

---

[341]Wimber, 1983, Tape 8.

[342]Dunn, 1975, 252.

[343]Fee, 1987, 622.

[344]Ibid., 622.

[345]Wimber, 1985c, 7.

[346]Wimber, 1985d, Tape 8.

[347]Clinton, 1998, 148.

in the Lord to those in need".[348] To summarize: Wimber treats *kybernesis* as "leadership" and *proistamenos* as "aid."

Gifted equippers (offices) / Gifted equippers

Wimber does not give a definition of this category, but simply calls it the gifted equippers (offices) of Ephesians 4. One common denominator of these gifted equippers (offices) is that they all (perhaps with the exception of evangelist) consist of several gracelets. In verse 12 we find the purpose of the function of the gifted equippers: to "prepare God's people for works of service." It is also crucial to note the context of this taxonomy: "The gifted equippers of Ephesians 4:11 are also to have the godly character of Ephesians 4:1–6 and Ephesians 4:17–32 with a track record of relating the truth of God's Word to the needs of their lives".[349]

Wimber then goes on to define each function; Apostle, Prophet, Pastor (-teacher), and Evangelist. I will only briefly present Wimber's definitions of each function but look closer at the gifted equipper (office) of Apostle since that currently is the most debated, and since a dynamic understanding has strong implications for this *charisma.*

Gordon Fee suggests, commenting on 1 Corinthians 12:28, that *Apostolos* are not to be taught of as "gifted equippers (offices)" held by "persons" in the local church, but rather as "ministries"—equals "function" in Wimber's terminology—that find expression in various persons".[350]

Apostolic function – apostles and Apostles

Wimber defines "apostle" like this:

> An apostle is one sent forth by God to introduce the gospel into new areas. This introduction is attended by signs and wonders which confirm the gospel. The work of an apostle is laying the foundation for the planting of new churches. A part of the task is building up the body by nurturing the converts.[351]

A few years later he distinguished between the broad sense "apostle" as used in 2 Corinthians 8:23 and John.13:16, and the restrictive sense of

---

[348]Wimber, 1985b, 29.
[349]Wimber, 1997b, 11.
[350]Fee, 1987, 619.
[351]Wimber, 1985b, 16.

"Apostle" in Mark.3:13–19 and Mark.10:1–4. He offers these definitions:

> An apostle (little "a") is one sent forth to win souls and make disci-
> ples, plant and nurture churches, and set things right in churches in
> which they had spiritual authority. This was often attended by signs
> and wonders.
>
> Apostle (with big "A") would include all the characteristics of apos-
> tle (with little "a"), plus these Apostles were specifically commis-
> sioned by Jesus (Acts 1:2–3 and Galatians 1:1), saw the resurrected
> Christ (Acts 1:22, 1 Corinthians 15:5–8), and some were used by
> God to write Scripture (Ephesians 3:5, 2 Peter 3:15). They ceased
> with the death of John, the last of the Twelve, and are the ones who
> will rule in heaven.[352]

The Greek word *apostolos* which is translated from the Hebrew word
shaliach, means "sent out," or "ambassador." Based on Luke 9:1–2 Wimber
describes the apostles' ministry as three-fold, since they had authority to
"expel demons . . . heal the sick . . . [and] preach the Kingdom of God".[353]
He further saw four main characteristics:

1.   They are called by God (Galatians 1:1,15).

2.   They are singled out by the church (Acts 13:1–3).

3.   They are recognized by the church (Galatians 2:7–10).

4.   They are confirmed by signs (2 Corinthians 12:12).[354]

Do we have apostles today? Is this *charisma* now limited to the gracelet
and ministry levels, or do we find Christian leaders holding the gifted
equipper (office) of apostle today? These are fundamental questions regarding apostles, which receive diverse answers. Only in certain denominational circles is it appropriate to speak of, and even less to seek, the gifted
equipper (office) of apostle.

An essential factor in answers to these questions is whether the gifted
equipper (office) of apostle always has been limited to the twelve disciples
of Jesus, or whether there were other apostles in the early church. Oskar
Skarsaaune writes that the early church used the word apostle with two

---

[352]Wimber, 1997b, 11.
[353]Wimber, 1985b, 16.
[354]Ibid., 16.

different meanings; with a narrow meaning referring to "only the twelve and Paul," and with a more expanded meaning referring to "traveling missionaries . . . as already in Acts 14:4, 14:14, and later in Didache".[355] I think it is unquestionable that the twelve first apostles had a unique position and gifted equipper (office), but the evidence of other apostles in the early church is readily available in the New Testament. Paul argues for his apostleship in Galatians 1:1. Barnabas is called apostle in Acts 14:14, James in Acts 1:19, Silvanus (Silas) and Timothy in 1 Thessalonians 1:1, and 2:6, Epaphroditus in Philippians 2:15, and Andronicus and Junias (a woman) in Romans 16:7. The warnings against "false apostles" in 2 Corinthians 11:13 are also demonstrating that there must have been other legitimate true apostles than the twelve.

If we look at the church history, we find that many pioneer-missionaries had strong apostolic gifted equippers (offices). Molland holds that the traveling apostles disappeared during the second century,[356] but that "at the entrance to the Middle-ages . . . the 'apostle' label was resurrected as a name for the missionaries who planted the gospel in new people-groups".[357] Patrick went to Ireland,[358] Ansgar took the gospel to Scandinavia, Cyril and Methodius to the "Southern Slavs," Otto Von Bamberg to Pomerania, Hans Egede established the church among the Eskimos (Inuit) on Greenland, and Robert Morrison went to China.[359] Wimber also mentions Carey.[360]

David Cannistraci states: "the apostle is first and foremost a servant. All true ministry is a result of a heartfelt commitment to humbly lay aside one's own agenda and serve the Father".[361] He points out the relational nature of apostolic authority, and uses the flexible alterations of the leadership roles of the early church between the Apostles to demonstrate that:

> Apostolic authority is neither successional (that is, able to be permanently imparted at the will of man) nor hierarchical (composed of numerous layers of authority) in its basic nature. Instead,

---

[355]My translation, Oskar Skarsaune, 1994, 90.

[356]Cited in Ibid., 90.

[357]Ibid., 90.

[358]Ibid., 90.

[359]Wimber, 1985b, 16-17.

[360]Wimber, 1997b, 11.

[361]David Cannistraci, 1996, 146.

leadership and submission among apostles is fluid, relational and subject to change as the situation and the will of God may dictate.[362]

Many wanted to call Wimber an apostle while he lived, but he was not willing to take on that title, saying he was "just a fat man trying to get to heaven," but he would probably not have argued that he had a "small-letter" apostolic ministry/function. A dynamic view opens the possibility of apostolic gifting on a lower level that the gifted equipper (office) of apostle, a concept which many have greater trouble with than Wimber.

Prophets, Evangelist, Pastors (pastor-teachers) and Teachers

Besides apostles, Ephesians 4:7–16 names four other "gifted equippers" who are given to the church. Wimber defines the gifted equipper called prophet (see above how he distinguishes between Old Testament and New Testament prophets) as:

> One through whom the gift of prophecy is consistently manifested. This person is used by God to communicate what God wants the community to hear concerning a specific situation. He/she is a spokesman for the Sprit, receiving direct revelation from God.[363]

Wimber defines the Evangelist as:

> One who proclaims the simple message of salvation to those who are non-believers with the effective result that men and women become disciples of Jesus and responsible parts of the Body of Christ.[364]

Wimber defines the gifted equipper, called pastor, as

> One who keeps watch over the flock and provides for their spiritual needs by leading, feeding, and protecting the sheep put under his care (Hebrews 13:17, 1 Timothy 5:17, Acts 20:28). A pastor does this through hard work, admonishing with God's Word, and modeling a godly life because he will give an account to God for this responsibility (1 Thessalonians 5:12–12, Hebrews 13:7, 17).[365]

---

[362]Ibid., 145.
[363]Wimber, 1997b, 12.
[364]Ibid, 12.
[365]Wimber, 1997b, 12.

Wimber defines Teacher as:

> One who provides for the spiritual needs of the flock by accurately unfolding the mysteries of the Word and relating them to the needs, opportunities, and mysteries of life. Teachers don't just tell but train the Body to think like the Bible writers so their thinking processes will be transformed to become more like Christ (Romans 12:1–2, 1 Corinthians 2:9–16).[366]

---

[366]Ibid., 12.

3: BIBLICAL THEOLOGICAL ANALYSIS OF WIMBER'S THEOLOGY

The Dynamic Aspects of Wimber's Theology of Charismata

In this chapter, I will attempt to provide a theological analysis of the dynamic labels of Wimber's theology of *charismata*. This will not be a complete exegesis but will focus on the aspects relevant to Wimber's dynamic aspects.

WORD-STUDY OF *CHARISMATA*

The main words Paul uses to refer to spiritual gifts are *charismata* and *pneūmatika*. I will also look briefly at the expression "Christ's gift."

Charisma

The root of the word *charisma*, which is translated "spiritual gift" in Romans 12:6 and 1 Corinthians 12:9, is *charis*, which means grace. The *ma* ending indicates that this is something concrete, to be touched, a particular manifestation of God's grace (1 Peter 4:10f).[367]

Paul also uses the expression in a wider meaning referring to God's saving grace, especially in Romans (Romans 5.15, 5:16, 6:23). Nevertheless, in a narrower sense the word is used to refer to particular gifts given by the Holy Spirit to believers in the congregation. Bauer defines the meaning of *charisma* as a "gift (freely and graciously given), a favor bestowed" and points out that in the New Testament it refers only to "gifts of divine

---

[367]Hvalvik, 1988, 86.

grace".[368] Strong defines it as "divine gratuity."[369]

Dunn describes grace (*charis*) as "a dynamic concept—the act of God for, in, and through man . . . it overlaps with the concepts of 'power' and 'spirit.' Indeed, it is often more or less synonymous with these terms", and it ranges from saving grace to the "actual, visible outworking of divine grace in a particular manifestation".[370]

He translates *charisma* as "the experience of grace coming to particular expression through an individual believer in some act or word usually for the benefit of others".[371] He does not distinguish between "acts of ministry and regular ministries," what Wimber called the gracelet and ministry levels:

> *Charisma* in Paul properly means a particular expression of *charis* (grace), some particular act of service, some particular activity, some particular manifestation of the Spirit. It is an event, not an aptitude, a transcendent gift given in and for a particular instance, not a human talent or ability always "on tap".[372]

Spittler, who coined the term "gracelet," suggests that it is not the gifts themselves that are situational manifestations, but that it is "the use of gifts that are situational manifestations of the Holy Spirit".[373] Dunn displays an even more dynamic view of how this is acted out:[374]

> It is for each member to recognize when and what *charisma* it is that the Spirit would bring to expression through him. And he must cooperate with the Spirit in bringing that *charisma* to expression, otherwise the functioning of the whole body will be impaired.[375]

Turner argues that *charisma* is derived from *charizomay* and not from

---

[368]Bauer, 1979, 878.

[369]Strong, # 5486). Deliverance (from danger or passion); (specifically) a (spiritual) endowment, i.e. (subjectively) a religious qualification, or (objectively) miraculous faculty.

[370]Dunn, 1975, 204.

[371]Dunn, 1990, 191.

[372]Ibid., 111.

[373]Spittler, 1999.

[374]It will be a too long sidetrack to enter into the implications this has for Dunn's view of ecclesiastical gifted equippers (offices) and the pastoral letters. For a critique of these implications, see Turner, 1998, 281-3.

[375]Dunn, 1990, 110.

charis (grace),[376] and that the *ma* ending means "result of" not "event of".[377] The correct meaning then is not "event of grace" but "gift," "thing (graciously) given," or "favor bestowed," and not "short term event".[378] He also points out that *charisma* does not have "any privileged (linguistic) relation to 'Spirit;' it does not have the specific sense 'spiritual gifts,' even when it refers to such".[379] If this is correct, it is a strong argument against the punctual aspect of *charisma*. This would weaken the case for the gracelet level in Wimber's model.

All respected English Bible translations translate *charismata* with "spiritual gifts" or "gifts of the Spirit," while the Norwegian translations use *nådegaver* ("grace-gifts"). This Norwegian translation specifies, "these are gifts given to people who do not deserve them," but does not connect the gifts to the Holy Spirit.

I am not able to determine whether Turner's rather unique suggestion reflects the correct translation, but if it does, it weakens Wimber's basis for the gracelet-element in his model. I choose to stick with the traditional understanding of *charisma* as a concrete manifestation of grace which usually is connected to power and the Spirit.

Pneūmatika

Pneūmatika is a parallel expression for *charisma* only Paul uses. Luke does not use it. The root of the word is *pneuma*, which means wind or breath or spirit. Bauer defines *pneūmatika* as "spiritual things or matters," and *pneūmatikos* as "pertaining to the spirit, spiritual".[380] The *tikos* ending is plural neutral and refers probably to "people"[381] or "things."[382] There is no word in Greek for "gift" here. *Pneūmatika* is only linked to *charisma* in Romans 1.11.

---

[376]See *Modern Linguistics*, Turner n.d.,146-74, 155-65.

[377]Turner, 1996, 264

[378]Ibid., 265-267.

[379]Ibid., 267.

[380]Bauer, 1979, 678-9.

[381] 3:1 – "people," and 2:13 – "one's".

[382]Strong defines *pneūmatikos* (# 4152) as non-carnal, i.e. (humanly ethereal (as opposed to gross), or (demonically) a spirit (concretely), or (divinely) supernatural, regenerate, religious.

Concerning its meaning in 1 Corinthians 12:1 Spittler suggests that it means "the spirituals," not spiritual gifts. Dunn discusses with himself if it refers to "spiritual men" (masculine) or "spiritual gifts" (neutral) and prefers the latter. But why does Paul mention those who say, "Jesus be cursed" (anathema – damned) here? We also see that there are no variations saying, "Christ be cursed." It is likely that these are the same people who are saying, "I follow Christ" in 1 Corinthians 1. Spittler therefore thinks that this refers to charismatics who were not interested in the bodily Jesus, only in the spiritual Christ. A likely motivation for this Gnostic confession was the fact that the Romans were killing people who confessed, "Jesus is Lord."

Concerning the meaning of *pneūmatika* in general, is it interesting to note that translating it as "spiritual things or matters" instead of "spiritual gifts" increases the probability of the correctness of Wimber's model. "Spiritual things and matters" indicate a more flexible, dynamic and "floating" understanding of how the Holy Spirit distributes gracelets than the permanent possession suggested by "spiritual gifts."

CHRIST'S GIFT

The expression "*tēs dōreas tu Christu*" (nominative: *tō dōrea to Christos*—Christ's gifts) is used in Ephesians 4:7 for the grace given each believer in the congregation. This expression highlights that all the gifts are meant to honor and glorify Christ. Riiser suggests that the "best way to test the reliability of a message/revelation, is to ask to what extent it glorifies Christ".[383] Riiser also holds that the verses which follow (verse 9–10) connect these gifts to Christ's "salvation economy, not to his creation economy".[384] The parable of the talents can be mentioned as reference for defining spiritual gifts as Christ's own resources and tools, which are transferred to and distributed in the congregation.

THE *CHARISMATA*-TAXONOMIES

Spittler describes Paul's *charismata* lists as: "taxonomy, lists arranged by

---

[383]My translation, Riiser, 1970, 26.
[384]Ibid., 26.

names".[385] Most theologians agree that these lists are not exhaustive, but few agree on which of the gifts in Paul's lists are for today and which other gifts should be included.[386] As we can see from the following figure, there is some overlapping between the various taxonomies.

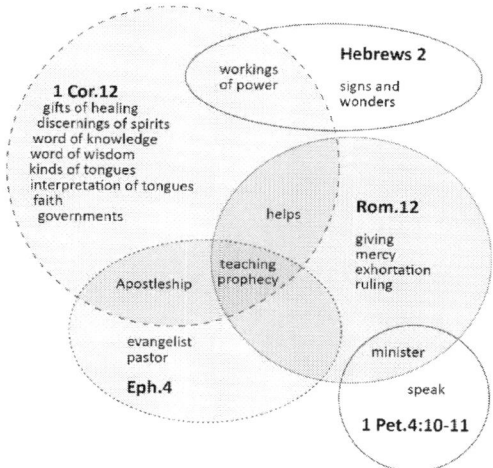

F6: Venn Diagram of Charismata-Taxonomies (Clinton and Clinton, 1998)

I will now comment briefly on the main taxonomies: Romans 12:6–8, 1 Corinthians 12:7–11, 1 Corinthians 12:27–31 and Ephesians 4:11–12. To make it easier to spot the particular *charisma* I have underlined them in the Scripture quotations.

Romans 12

The primary text on spiritual gifts in Romans is 12:6–8. As a part of a section with "practical exhortations" (12:1–15:13), chapter 12 reviews some "general duties." Guthrie summarizes verse 3–8: "Christians are to learn to develop a sober estimate of themselves".[387]

---

[385]Spittler, 1999.

[386]Various theological schools display great diversion when it comes to the number of gifts. Some of these variations are because some are only post-Pentecost, not in the gospels, and some include the Old Testament. A few examples are: Wagner, 27; Hummel, 21; Wimber, 20 + 10 possible; McRae, 18 in Bible, only 9 today; T. Blanchard, 13; D. Gee, 9; R. Clinton and R & J Clinton, 19.

[387]Guthrie, 1990, 431.

> We have different gifts, according to the grace given us. If a man's gift is prophesying, let him use it in proportion to his faith. If it is serving, let him serve; if it is teaching, let him teach; if it is encouraging, let him encourage; if it is contributing to the needs of others, let him give generously; if it is leadership, let him govern diligently, if it is showing mercy, let him do it cheerfully (Romans 12:6–8).

Richard Clinton points out that this passage differs from 1 Corinthians because here Paul is "not trying to solve problems. The purpose here is to show how to live the Christian life, and the central trust is to know yourself and minister in the gifts God has given you and develop them".[388] Obviously, this taxonomy is not complete either, but it deserves probably just as much attention as the taxonomies we find in 1 Corinthians 12. Except from prophecy, which is the only commonality with the lists in 1 Corinthians 12, Paul does not include any other "supernatural" or extraordinary gifts. This list has not surprisingly therefore been regarded by some non-charismatics and cessationists as the only correct list. They hold that these seven gifts are the only gifts that exist, at least today.[389]

1 Corinthians 12–14

The taxonomies in 1 Corinthians are placed in a section with instructions for public worship ranging from chapter 12 to 14, which is a part of a larger section dealing with the "problems raised by the Corinthians" (7:1–15:58).[390] Spittler calls the theme in chapter 12 "varied in nature," chapter 13 "loving in exercise," and chapter 14 "constructive in effect—ought to build up the community".[391] It seems like one group is demanding unity in terms of "everybody doing the same," and Paul's answer is to emphasize the need for diversity.[392]

> To each one the manifestation of the Spirit is given for the common good. To one there is given through the Spirit the message of wisdom, to another the message of knowledge by means of the same Spirit, to another faith by the same Spirit, to another miraculous

---

[388]Clinton, 1999.
[389]Clinton 2000.
[390]Guthrie, 1990, 461.
[391]Spittler, 1999.
[392]Clinton, 1999.

powers, to another prophecy, to another distinguishing between spirits, to another speaking in different tongues, and to still another the interpretation of tongues. All these are the work of the same Spirit, and he gives them to each one, just as he determines (1 Corinthians 12:7–11).

Earlier I commented on the phrase in verse 7, "to each one . . . is given," (see chapter 2). Many theologians treat this list as "the official complete list of spiritual gifts", but I will argue that this list is neither complete nor organized in any prioritized order. Fee makes the following observations:

> Paul's argument is entirely ad hoc, reflecting the Corinthian situation itself; therefore, his own concern is not with instruction about "spiritual gifts" as such, their number and kinds. Indeed, the list of nine items in verse 8–10 is neither carefully worked out nor exhaustive; it is merely representative of the diversity of the Spirit's manifestations. Paul's concern here is to offer a considerable list so that they will stop being singular in their own emphasis.[393]

Spittler suggests that Paul "starts out with the gifts the Corinthians are interested in (somebody is probably pounding on wisdom and tongues), and continues with some he coughs up".[394] Dunn thinks, "it was the value put on 'knowledge,' and 'wisdom' by the self-styled *pneumatikoi* (spiritual men) . . . Paul saw as the root of the problem in 1 Corinthians 1:17–4:21".[395]

The theme of this section is found in verse 4: "There are different kinds of gifts, but the same Spirit." Paul makes it very clear that all the different kinds of manifestations (verse 7); both the gifts (verse 4), the services/ministries (verse 5), and the workings (verse 6), come from the same Spirit. By interchangeably using "Lord" (verse 5), "God" (verse 6), and "Spirit" (verse 4), he shows that the diversity of *charismata* is rooted in the Triune God himself.[396]

At the end of the same chapter, we find another taxonomy which includes five of the *charismata* listed in verse 8–10 and three of the gifted equippers (offices) listed in Ephesians 4.

Now you are the body of Christ, and each one of you is a part of it.

---

[393]Fee 1987, 585.
[394]Spittler, 1999.
[395]Dunn, 197, 266.
[396]Fee, 1987, 586-588.

And in the Church God has appointed first of all apostles, second prophets, third teachers, then workers of miracles, also those having gifts of healing, those able to help others, those with gifts of administration, and those speaking in different kinds of tongues. Are all apostles? Are all prophets? Are all teachers? Do all work miracles? Do all have gifts of healing? Do all speak in tongues? Do all interpret? But eagerly desire the greater gifts. And now let me show you the most excellent way (1 Corinthians 12:27–31).

W. Harold Mare and Bittlinger believe that *zeloute* (desire) in verse 31 is not an imperative but rather an indicative,[397] and thereby a rebuke, and suggests that the correct translation is "But you are eagerly desiring the greater gifts." This translation creates a more logical introduction into chapter 13 where Paul "shows the right way to exercise all spiritual gifts— the way of love . . . [because] the Corinthians were apparently seeking status through the exercise of the gifts that seemed to them the more important".[398] Fee and Williams argue contrariwise that the normal translation seems correct because *zeloute* unquestionably is imperative in 1 Corinthians 14:1.[399] Fee thinks that it does not stand in contrast to 12:4–30, but says, "in the community all the intelligible gifts are 'greater' than tongues because they can edify".[400]

Ephesians 4

In Ephesians 4 Paul uses the word *doma* instead of *charisma*, but the meaning is, practically speaking, identical. Råmundal suggests that this expression characterizes the gifts from the congregation's point of view.[401]

It was He who gave some to be apostles, some to be prophets, some to be evangelists, and some to be pastors and teachers, to prepare God's people for works of service, so that the body of Christ might be built up (Ephesians 4:11–12).

This paragraph is a part of "a description of the diversity of gifts" (4:7–13),

---

[397]W. Harold Mare and Bittlinger, 1967, 73.
[398]Mare, 1985, 1752.
[399]Williams, 1990, 341 and Fee, 1987, 623-35, 654-55.
[400]Fee, 1987, 625.
[401]Råmundal, 1997, 160.

which is found in the "practical section" (4:1–6:17) of the epistle to the Ephesians.[402]

Clinton describes the *charismata* or gifted equippers (offices) in Ephesians as "leadership gifts," not gifted equippers (offices), and suggests adding two more, namely "administration" and "ruling." He points out that we "don't know whether [Paul] means the house church, the local church, the regional church, etc.",[403] and he thinks, "what is important for Paul is not the structure of the church," but that which he draws our attention to in verse 12—the result.

Pentecostal theology has focused on the "fivefold ministry" in this verse. More recently a restorationist theology has emerged among many charismatic leaders and writers, who believe that in the 40s the gifted equipper (office) of evangelist was given back to the church, in the 50s the gifted equipper (office) of pastor, in the 80s the prophetic gifted equipper (office), and in the 90s the apostolic gifted equipper (office).[404] Others have a somewhat longer perspective, and argue that pastors came after the Reformation, evangelists from the Great Awakenings onward, prophets in the 1980s, and that the apostles are yet to come.

ANALYSIS OF THE PUNCTUAL ASPECT OF *CHARISMA*

Wimber's theology of *charismata* inspires us to investigate whether the punctual aspect is the key to understanding Paul's description of the early church's experience of spiritual gifts. Tangen argues that this question is fundamental concerning whether all Christians can operate in the gift of healing—which is his area of study—and it is of equal importance for most other spiritual gifts. Dunn agrees with Wimber on the punctual nature of the Word of Knowledge, "it is a particular word given in a particular instance and is 'mine' only in the act and moment of uttering it".[405]

---

[402]Guthrie, 1990, 358.

[403]Clinton, 1999.

[404]See Peter Wagner, *The New Apostolic Paradigm Churches*, and David Cannistraci, *The Gift of Apostle*.

[405]Dunn, 1975, 221.

The Gospels

There are not many references to the Holy Spirit in Matthew or Mark. Tangen points out that it is "interesting that one of the few references to the Holy Spirit, very well can be interpreted in light of Wimber's punctual understanding of the spiritual gifts".[406] The passage Tangen refers to is Mark 13:11b, "Just say whatever is given you at the time, for it is not you speaking, but the Holy Spirit."

In Luke 11:13 we are encouraged to ask for the Holy Spirit. James Dunn considers whether this is this linked to the Christian initiation, and concludes it is probably not,[407] which makes it an encouragement to receive the Holy Spirit continuously. Engelsviken writes, on Acts 1.8, that it "can seem like the Spirit's dynamis is something that repeatedly is given again and again".[408] Bruce states, about Acts 4.8, that "the fact that the Greek participle is in aorist, underlines the punctual aspect, and suggests that Peter is filled there and then".[409] Based on these examples one can safely conclude that the punctual aspect of the Holy Spirit's work is represented at least in Acts.

Tangen argues that "John 14:12 fits with Wimber, everybody can pray for the sick. In John 5:5ff, and 5:19 it is very possible that the Father punctually shows Jesus whom to heal," and asks if this is meant to be prescriptive for the church?[410] He concluded, "healings and wonders are something that is given again and again".[411] Dunn contrasts what he describes as an "immediate relationship" to the ministry/gifted equipper (office):

> In short, throughout these writings there is no real concept of ministry, let alone gifted equipper (office). Everything is seen through the individual's immediate relationship to God through the Spirit and the Word.[412]

---

[406]Tangen, 1993, 107.

[407]Dunn, 1970, 33, 53.

[408]Engelsviken, 1981, 78-80.

[409]Bruce, 1988, 92.

[410]Tangen, my translation, 1993, 109.

[411]My translation, Ibid.

[412]Dunn, 1990, 119.

Paul

Charisma is a distinctively Pauline word. It occurs sixteen times in the Pauline texts.[413] Throughout 1 Corinthians 12:1–10 Paul is most likely describing the gifts from a manifestation perspective.[414] This is clear from verse 7: "to each is given the manifestation of the Spirit." Hesselberg notes that the continuous tense of "give" in 1 Corinthians 12:7ff

> can mean that the gifts are of such a kind that they are being given again and again. The Spirit is manifesting himself repeatedly. In other words, that it is not gifts that are given to the individual once and for all, but that they are given repeatedly . . . This underlines that it is not we who manage the gifts, but the Spirit who manages us.[415]

They continue to point out that nobody can heal at will even if they have done it before; the Holy Spirit has to manifest himself to make it happen. This presents a potential contrast with the Clintons' model, where the healing gift can be "vested."[416]

Fee comments that Paul's "urgency, as verse 8–10 make clear, is not that each person is 'gifted,' but that the Spirit is manifested in a variety of ways".[417] Concerning the double plural in the expression "gifts of healings" he comments, "the plural *charismata* probably suggests not a permanent 'gift,' as it were, but that each occurrence is a 'gift' in its own right".[418] As I mentioned earlier, Bittlinger suggests that "every healing is a special gift— in this way the spiritually gifted individual stands always in new dependence upon the divine giver".[419]

The Pastoral Letters

Many theologians has expressed difficulties trying to reconcile the evidence of structured churches we find in the pastoral letters with the much more free, spontaneous and flexible exercising of spiritual gifts we see in

---

[413]The only occurrence outside of Paul comes from a "typical Pauline passage (1.Peter 4:10)". Dunn, 1975, 205.

[414]Tangen, 1993, 110.

[415]Hesselberg, et al, my translation, 1977, 135.

[416]See page 58.

[417]Fee, 1987, 589.

[418]Ibid., 594.

[419]Bittlinger, 1967, 37. See Chapter 2 concerning the recipients of gifts of healing.

Paul's letters to the Romans and especially to the Corinthians.

Rudolph Sohm argued in 1892 that all forms of permanent structures, as we see them in the pastoral letters, stand in strong opposition to Paul's ecclesiology.[420] He regarded the congregation in Corinth—where the Spirit blew where it wanted—as the genuine Pauline church structure. This school regards the pastoral letters as pre-Catholic and not genuine Pauline. As already noted, Wimber's model builds a bridge between these apparently opposing pictures; he views the gifted equippers (offices) we find in Ephesians as a natural development from the gracelets and ministries we see in Romans and Corinthians.

The Letters to Timothy

Perhaps the strongest argument against Wimber's punctual view is this command by Paul, which seems to assume that gifts permanently reside in the believer:

> Do not neglect your gift, which was given to you through a prophetic message when the body of elders laid their hands on you (1 Timothy 4:13–16).

Important factors to consider are firstly, that Paul is giving this command to Timothy, whom he knew well. He knew how and when he had been given this gift. This might not indicate that this is prescriptive for all gifts given to all believers. Wimber would have called this an impartation, an important element in his theology of *charismata*.[421]

Secondly, the fact that Paul tells him to not neglect the gift can be an indication that Timothy—at least in practical terms—may lose the gift if he does not use it and grow in it. The command can also be understood as an encouragement to Timothy, who clearly must have operated in several gifts, to focus on this particular gift, since God had revealed through a prophetic message that this was an important gift for his ministry.

The connected command in 2 Timothy 1:6 can also, at first sight, seem contradictory to Wimber's model. Paul is here urging Timothy to refresh/rekindle "the gift of God that is within you through the laying on of my hands." But it is clear from the context that it is unlikely that Paul is referring to a particular single gift, since Timothy was assigned to and

---

[420]Cited in Sandnes, 1996, 236.
[421]See Chapter 2.

equipped for a pastoral ministry of general oversight for the congregation in Ephesus (1 Timothy 1:3, 18f). In the following verse, Paul goes on to describe what kind of Spirit we have been given. These factors lead me to the conclusion that the expression "*charisma tu theu*" here must refer to the Holy Spirit himself, not a specific charismatic gift. It can be argued that it refers to "pastor," but since Paul only mentions "pastor" on the ministry/gifted equipper (office) level (Ephesians 4:11), this is not an argument against the punctual non-permanent nature of *charismata* on the gracelet level.

Hebrews and James

> God also testified by signs, wonders and various miracles, and gifts of the Holy Spirit distributed according to his will (Hebrews 2:4).

I suggest that this text has been wrongly translated in the NIV (and NB78) with "gifts of the Holy Spirit distributed" Since *charisma* is not mentioned here, I find it most likely that *merismois* (distributed) refers to *pnevmatos hagiu* (the Holy Spirit). Like NB88 I think the correct translation is "by giving/distributing the Holy Spirit according to his will" (my translation). If this is correct, it is the Holy Spirit who is distributed, not more or less permanent gifts—which would weaken the case for Wimber's view.

Martin Dibelius[422] sees a disconnection between the elders' responsibility to pray for the sick in James 5:14–15 and 1 Corinthians 12, but sees a traditional-historical[423] connection to Mark 11:22. Based on this, Tangen makes the interesting suggestion that the elders could expect the Holy Spirit to give them the gift of faith when they are ministering to sick persons.

1 Peter

> Each one should use whatever gift he has received to serve others, faithfully administrating God' grace in its various forms. If anybody speaks (*lalei*), he should do it as one speaking the very words of God. If anyone serves (*diakonei*), he should do it with the strength God

---

[422]Martin Dibelius, 1964, 233.
[423]*Tradisjonshistorisk.*

provides (1 Peter 4:10–11).

At first sight, this verse does not seem to harmonize with Wimber's view, since it indicates that each one has received one gift. In the NIV translation two "gifts" are mentioned: to speak (*laleō*) and to serve (*diakoneō*). *Laleō* is compared to "God's very words"[424] in 4:11, but both these words can also refer to everyday acts which everyone is, or should be, doing. I would therefore suggest that the phrase "the *charisma* each has been given," here refers to "the grace each has been given."

I am aware that this goes against the most common interpretation, but I find it possible that the first part of 4:10 can be translated like this: "Each one should use the amount of grace he has received to serve others". If this interpretation is correct the meaning of the paragraph will be to live our normal Christian lives receiving and distributing God's grace by our words and deeds, by what we say and do. This understanding comes close to what Wimber called "roles".[425]

GENERAL COMMENTS AND SUMMARY

Tangen agrees with Wimber's emphasis of the manifestation aspect, but writes, "Wimber's theology of spiritual gifts does not come to terms with the wholeness in the Pauline lists of spiritual gifts",[426] and refers to Engelsviken who writes that:

> Through comparing lists of charisms one notices that there are references not only to events, but also to persons, not only to spontaneous acts of power, but also to permanent unspectacular ministries, not only to inspired speech, but also to premeditated instructions.[427]

Tangen's point is: "Ephesians 4 and Romans 12 do not divide between 'gift' understood as manifestation and service, . . . '*charisma*' as preaching and more permanent practical services in 1 Peter 2:5 . . . [And in] 1 Corinthians 12:4–7 . . . both parts are understood as '*pneūmatika*'". He concludes

---

[424]The Greek phrase for this is also used in Acts 7:38 and Romans 3:2 referring to the Scriptures or words God has spoken.

[425]See Chapter 2.

[426]My translation, Tangen, 1993,111.

[427]Engelsviken, 1981, 506.

therefore that Wimber's manifestation aspect is correct concerning some gifts, but that there also are "permanent services independent of the manifestations".[428]

This comment suggests that he has only looked at half of Wimber's model and is not aware of the encouragement in Wimber's model to develop from the manifestation-level to the ministry and gifted equipper levels.

The punctual aspect of the Holy Spirit's activity is present in both Matthew, Mark, and Acts, and the notion of gracelets finds a good basis in John. I found the manifestation aspect central in Paul's descriptions of spiritual gifts and think that Wimber's model builds a bridge between the apparently contradictory pictures Paul draws in the pastoral letters and the rest of his writings.

---

[428]Tangen, 1993, 111.

4: APPLICATIONS FOR DEVELOPING *CHARISMATA*

> If the charism of individual Christians were discovered and fur-
> thered and developed, what dynamic power, what life and move-
> ment there would be in such a community, such a church (Hans
> Kung).[429]

A dynamic view of spiritual gifts opens up the possibility that gifts can be developed. I will now look at ways this can be done through teaching, training, and experience. Since Wimber did not publish any teaching concerning the development of gifts, I will base this chapter on a few scholars who have all interacted extensively with Wimber and his model: Jack Deere, Peter Wagner, and Robert Clinton. I will also use Richard Clinton, who served as a Vineyard pastor. It must be kept in mind that Wimber was very much against,

> Believing that Spiritual Gifts are under the control of the gifted.
> "Discover YOUR spiritual gifts and YOU can USE it" is an errone-
> ous concept. Gifts are not discovered, they are imparted (2 Timothy
> 1:6).[430]

However, this does not automatically imply that spiritual gifts cannot be cultivated through teaching, training, and experience. Deere refers to people having a "difficult time understanding how you can cultivate or develop a gift that is supernaturally empowered," and suggest that:

> This difficulty stems from viewing the miraculous gifts as magical
> or mechanical. A teacher can grow in the gift of teaching and an
> evangelist can grow in their gift of evangelism. Why is it difficult to
> believe that someone can grow in the gift of healing or prophecy?

---

[429]Kung, 1967, C, II, 3.
[430]Wimber, 1985a, 3.

> The truth is that we all can grow in every spiritual exercise and every spiritual gift.[431]

Cooperating with what God is doing in one's life and cultivating for gifts is undoubtedly in accordance with Wimber's strong desire to equip normal Christians to be used supernaturally by the Holy Spirit in everyday life. I will therefore provide some suggestions on how to develop different gifts, but first there are a few foundational questions which need to be dealt with.

IS *CHARISMA* AN ENHANCEMENT OF NATURAL TALENTS?

Spittler asks if spiritual gifts are "an enhancement of a talent or external inducement?" He thinks it is both, because he does not "doubt that natural talents can be endowed," and says that we "can't standardize the Spirit".[432] One the one hand, there is the view that a *charisma* is an enhancement of a natural talent. Bittlinger writes: "A gift is manifested when being set free by the Holy Spirit, natural talents blossom forth glorifying Christ and building up His church".[433] On the other hand, there is the view that all the gifts are basically supernatural, and accordingly,

> are not latent natural talents or trained abilities brought to a heightened expression. The spiritual gifts are by no means more of what is already present, no matter how elevated. They are not simply an added spiritual injection that causes talents and abilities to function with greater effectiveness or transposes them to a higher level. They are gifts of the Spirit, endowments, not enhancements—apportionments of the Holy Spirit.[434]

Since Wimber's emphasis is on the dynamic aspects of operating in spiritual gifts, he pedagogically limits his scope to external inducement:

> One thing that may have prevented us from asking for the gifts is that we have been taught that they are related to personality traits. God does give us our unique personalities, so they are, in that sense, gifts from God. But spiritual gifts as I am discussing them are

---

[431]Deere, 1993, 165.

[432]Spittler, 1999.

[433]Bittlinger, 1967, 72.

[434]Williams, 1990, 332.

independent of personality traits.[435]

WHY IS IT IMPORTANT TO DISCOVER YOUR *CHARISMATA*?

Grudem puts the responsibility for developing of gifts on the leaders of the church, who "need to ask whether they are providing sufficient opportunities for varieties of gifts to be used".[436]

Gene Getz disagrees with the idea that Christians should discover their *charisma*. He cannot find, anywhere in the gift-taxonomies, "any exhortation for individual Christians to 'look for' or 'try to discover' their spiritual gift or gifts".[437] He provides three reasons, while emphasizing "body maturity": faith, hope, love, and the leadership qualities in 1 Timothy 3 and Titus 1.[438]

1. *Confusion.* Teaching Christians to discover spiritual gifts they received at conversion has, in fact, caused many people, even mature believers, to become confused.

2. *Rationalization.* Some tend to fix their attention on a supposed gift and use it as a rationalization for not fulfilling other Biblical responsibilities. For example, some may say they have the gift of pastoring, but not teaching. Or others might say they do not have the gift of evangelism because they feel uncomfortable sharing Christ.

3. *Self-deception.* Some people think they have a spiritual gift when they really do not.[439]

All these three arguments can actually just as well be used to argue for Wimber's dynamic and punctual understanding of *charismata*. I agree, on 1 above, that it can be difficult to discover which gift you are presently ministering in if you need to review your whole Christian life based, and assuming that you have had the same gift since your conversion. I have already mentioned argument 2 as one of Wimber's concerns. Argument 3

---

[435]Wimber, 1991, 148-9.
[436]Grudem, 1994, 1028.
[437]Gene Getz, 1976, 9-16.
[438]Wagner, 1996, 37.
[439]Gets, 1976, 9-16.

has merit, since it advises people not to focus too strongly on a particular gift before the gracelet is occurring frequently enough for leaders and co-ministers to confirm it as a ministry.

Grudem thinks, "Paul seems to assume that believers will know what their spiritual gifts are",[440] and Clinton believes, "all are expected to assess what capacity God has given them. [And all] must be humble and agree with God".[441] Wagner states: "one of the primary spiritual exercises for any Christian is to discover, develop and use his or her spiritual gift".[442] He defends the appropriateness of trying to discover spiritual gifts by referring to what he sees as a "clear Biblical relationship between 'having gifts' (Romans 12.6), 'thinking soberly about yourself' (verse 3) and doing the 'good and acceptable and perfect will of God' (verse 2)".[443] O'Connor points out that this is a crucial way to learn God's will for one's life and ministry.

We seek the will of God without assuming that it is written into our very beings. We perceive his will as we discern our gifts.[444]

As mentioned earlier, Wimber was against a technical attempt to determine/discover one's gift. For him, *charismata*

are not discovered by research or study, but sovereignly given by God's grace through us to others.[445]

This is an adamant statement against non-charismatic spiritual gifts tests that focus on personal traits/talents. In Wimber's model, discovery/determination of one's *charismata* must be experience-based, and consist of systemizing and analyzing the Holy Spirit's activity through oneself.

WHY DEVELOP YOUR *CHARISMATA*?

Paul encourages us to "Eagerly desire the spiritual gifts, especially the gift of prophecy" (1 Corinthians 14.1). This implies that we are to to seek and ask for stronger and more gifts. Grudem understands the repeated use of *meizon* (higher or greater) in 1 Corinthians 12.31 (based on in 14:5), as an

---

[440]Grudem, 1994, 1028.
[441]Clinton, 1999.
[442]Wagner, 1996, 36.
[443]Ibid.
[444]O'Connor, 1971, 15.
[445]Wimber, 1985c, 5.

encouragement to seek those gifts "that build up the church more and bring more benefit to others".[446]

Although Wimber, due to his emphasis on the *charismata* not being resident, is antagonistic to the idea of developing *charismata* as if they were skills, he clearly thinks that there is potential for growth and development. His approach was to focus on sensitivity towards the Holy Spirit.

> These are delicate nuances in our relationship with God, and we have to be sensitive enough to respond to them. If we do not, we will never learn to move in the power of the Holy Spirit.[447]

A related approach is to focus on developing "the capacity to be used, put yourself in a place where you can be used, practice intimacy with God" (Spittler 1999). Spittler also reminds us of a crucial motivation: "We should not be seeking gifts as much as seeking to show love through the gifts we have".[448]

I agree with Clinton that instead of focusing on the power, strength, or the effect of a *charisma* in comparison to another ministry, the goal must be to develop one's gifts to its full potential. He suggests that we should start by gaining "knowledge of what the gift looks like when it's mature" (Clinton 1999). However, what does such maturity look like? Clinton defines maturity as follows:

> Abilities, skills, and gifts are operating in harmony and synergy. The parts of the Venn diagram merge, connect, and flow together. Get into roles we fit in . . . Often can't distinguish between the parts.[449]

"Focused life" is the Clinton's label on the final stage of a minister's life. They define it as "operating in maximum potential, accomplishing God's purposes, finishing well."

WHO IS RESPONSIBLE FOR DEVELOPING ONE'S *CHARISMATA*?

Richard Clinton thinks that it is a part of every leader's mandate to reproduce oneself. He asks, "have you ever seen a teacher who tries to train a

---

[446]Grudem, 1994, 1029.
[447]Wimber, 1991, 148.
[448]Spittler, 1999.
[449]Clinton, 1999.

prophet?" and points out that evangelists should produce evangelists, and so on.[450] He places the main responsibility for developing the gift on the gifted person himself.

> Vested gifts carry with them the responsibility for development and the realization that you will held accountable for the use of them in ministry.[451]

When Christ calls leaders to Christian ministry, he intends to develop them to their full potential. Each of us in leadership is responsible to continue developing in accordance with God's processes in our lives.[452]

He points out that since we "don't know our potential, . . . keep developing until you reach it. You'll know when you get to heaven how close you got".[453]

Wimber seems to place more of the responsibility on the leaders, since "the Vineyard concept of training is apprenticeship, not education or teaching".[454] What you see is what you become. Wimber encouraged the pastors to be visible models, modeling the "key ministries and practices within the Church".[455] "Who or what we model, as leaders, will influence our people and form our Church—for better or for worse!" This will demand thoughtful consideration by those to whom leadership and public exposure are given.

Compared to tight discipleship-models with heavy submission expectancies, Wimber's understanding of discipleship was "that we are being apprenticed by Jesus, learning directly from him and through one another".[456]

Wimber encouraged leaders to create a "climate of risk taking"[457] where it is safe to try and fail. Alexander Venter believes, "such training happens primarily in the context of ongoing relationships—most practically through home groups and ministry groups," but mentions also big gatherings, field ministries, and semi-formal settings like seminars, courses, and

---

[450]Clinton, 1999.
[451]Clinton and Clinton, 1998, 130.
[452]Clinton, 1999.
[453]Clinton, 1999.
[454]Venter, 2000, 173.
[455]Ibid., 174.
[456]Ibid., 173.
[457]Wimber, 1985c, 5.

conferences with "clinic" or "ministry time" where practice can take place.[458]

THE "SHOW AND TELL" METHOD OF TRAINING

Based on the concept of apprenticeship/modeling, Wimber promoted a general teaching model, which has been called the "show and tell" method or the "four step model." The method can most easily be described like this:

1. The mentoree watches the mentor do it,

2. The mentoree works alongside the mentor,

3. The mentoree does it while the mentor watches and guides, and

4. The mentoree does it by herself or himself.

He describes the result of having people exposed to a model like this:

> The gifts . . . are developed in a climate of risk-taking and willingness to fail. The way to teach people is to have them exposed to a model. They can "see it," "hear it," and then "try it." They can "think about it," have it "reinforced" and "try again." Finally, they will "be it" and "do it" for the rest of their life.[459]

Venter lays out the method in more detail.

1. You model it (do the ministry with the others watching).

2. Then you talk about it (reflect on what happens, answer the questions that are raised because of what is seen and experienced).

3. Then you get them to do it (do it as you did it, while you watch them).

4. Then you talk about it (feed back to them your observations and discuss the questions that will arise from their doing it).

5. Then you repeat the process (as often as is needed for them to "catch it").

---

[458]Venter, 2000, 175.
[459]Wimber, 1985c, 5.

6. Then you leave them doing it (monitor and encourage them).

7. Finally you get them to repeat the same process with others.[460]

This emphasis on teaching and modeling explains why Wimber did not conduct more "on stage" healing ministry. He preferred doing it more low-key, in front of the stage. He wanted to use a model that was easier to copy for normal people. On stage ministry tends to create a division between the audience and the expert.

He often asked specific people whom he saw the Holy Spirit dwelling on, or everybody who felt this themselves, to come forward to receive ministry. Ministry teams would pray for people, but he might also give an open invitation to come forward to help pray, or ask those wanting prayer to stand up in the aisles and ask the people around them to minister to them. The reason why this worked is that his primarily approach to ministering/praying for people was to "bless what God is doing." It is not necessary to be a trained counselor or prayer-partner to simply "bless what God is doing" or ask the "Holy Spirit to come and heal." Wimber determined whom the Holy Spirit was resting on by looking for manifestations (such as shaking, heavy breathing, rapidly moving eyelids, crying, etc.—which everybody can see in order to "bless what God is doing"), as well as by discerning by the Holy Spirit.

HOW CAN *CHARISMATA* BE DEVELOPED?

There are two sides to this question. Both must be addressed to release gifts in the congregation. The congregation must be structured for gifts, and the members must be helped to focus on appropriate gifts. Further, Wimber writes, the following "five steps which Dr. Wagner affirms provide valuable insights for those desiring a ministry which includes Signs and Wonders".[461]

Step 1. Agree on a philosophy of ministry.

Step 2. Initiate a growth process—Room is made within the church for the gracelets of God to operate as he guides.

---

[460]Venter, 2000, 175.
[461]Wimber, 1985c, 6.

Step 3. Structure for gifts and growth. It is here that the equipping of the saints for the ministry takes place. This is not education, i.e. learning more information about gracelets. This is equipping, i.e. the actual doing of the gifts.

Step 4. Unwrap the spiritual gifts by:

1. Motivating the community by instruction,

2. Encouraging them to study the Biblical teaching concerning gifts,

3. Helping them to release the gifts, and

4. Using the gifts within a new ongoing lifestyle.

Step 5. Expect God's blessing.[462]

On the personal level, Grudem suggests that believers, who do not know what their spiritual gifts are, start out by asking, "what gifts are most needed for the building up of the church at this point?".[463] He further suggests that they "do some self-examination," by looking for "interests and desires and abilities," "advice and encouragement" from others, "blessing in the past in ministering in a particular kind of service." He also points out how important it is to "pray and ask God for wisdom," and to "simply begin to try ministering in various areas and see where God brings blessing".[464] The Clintons recommend gaining ministry experience, as well as getting mentoring from someone who operates in the specific gift you want to develop.[465]

Deere lists seven factors he personally found helpful to cultivate the gifts of the Spirit:

1. Be convinced that the Bible teaches the gifts are for today and that they are important; otherwise you won't have faith to exercise them or to pray for them. Likewise, you must be confident that the gifts are given to all Christians (1 Peter 4:10) rather than just a few specially deserving people.

---

[462]Wagner, 1979, 243-258 cited in Wimber, 1985c, 6-7.

[463]Grudem, 1994, 1028.

[464]Ibid., 1029.

[465]Clinton and Clinton, 1998, 256-291.

2. I have attempted to use them on a regular basis.

3. Study the gifts (the Scriptures, books, bibliographies).

4. Having friendships with people who are more advanced in the gifts than I am.

5. Have a non-threatening atmosphere when you begin to practice the gifts of the Spirit.

6. Conferences on spiritual gifts.

7. Finally, as you are learning about spiritual gifts, be patient . . . the Holy frustration you feel right now is meant to drive you on.[466]

Pattern of Development of Giftedness by Various Means

A foundational value I share with Clinton and Clinton,[467] is to first analyze ministry experience instead of interests and personality traits, when attempting to "discover" which gifts to focus on. This form of "discovery" is helpful to remember and summarize which gracelets God has let you minister in previously. This model is much easier to reconcile with Wimber's dynamic principles, since the aim is not to discover "the gifts you have been in possession of since you received the Holy Spirit," but rather to discover continuums of gracelets that form a ministry.

Based on research conducted by Grounded Theory, the Clintons have discovered a pattern of how giftedness usually develops.

---

[466]Deere, 1993, 165-169.
[467]Clinton and Clinton, 1998.

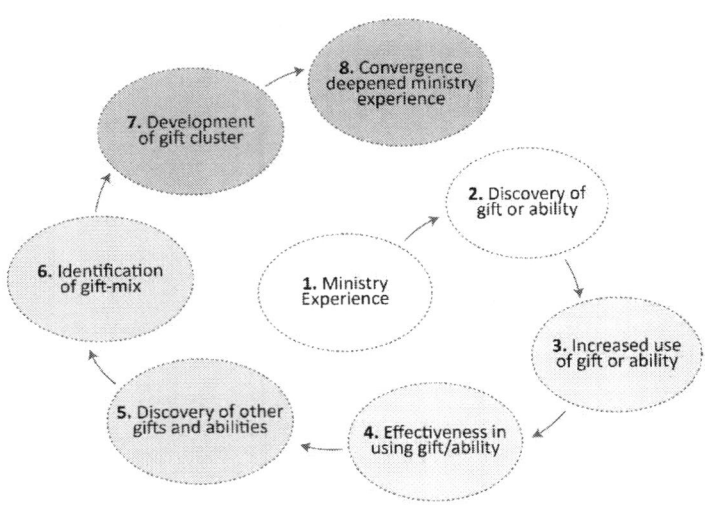

F7: Giftedness Development Pattern (Clinton and Clinton, 1998, 253)

One term in this figure that might need explanation is "gift cluster." The Clintons define this as "a person's gift mix which has matured in such a way that one gift is dominant, and the other gifts harmonize with that gift in order to maximize the person's effectiveness".[468]

In order to reach one's potential it is crucial to utilize all available means for developing the various gifts. The various means for developing can be grouped in three categories:

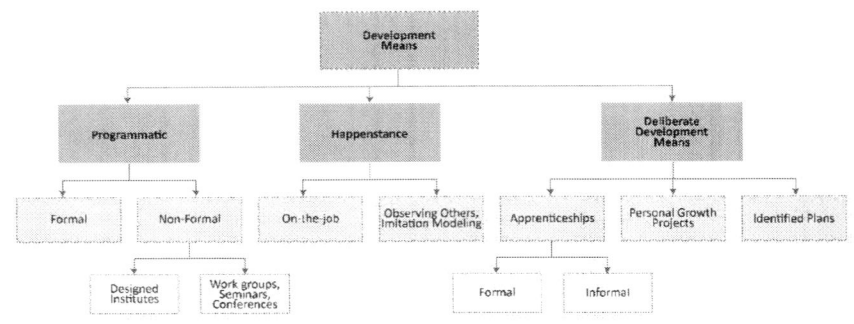

F8: Development Means (Clinton and Clinton, 1998, 255)

---

[468]Ibid., 46.

1. Programmatic means (designed training),

2. Happenstance means (day-to-day learning in the normal course of life's activities and processes), and

3. Deliberate Development means (disciplined self-initiated learning).[469]

Suggestions for Developing Specific Gifts

To go into detail about methods for developing various gifts would be outside the scope of this thesis. The Clinton's *Unlocking Your Giftedness* does this quite extensively, covering eighteen gifts.[470] They provide detailed suggestions for Bible study, related skills and abilities to develop, bibliographies portraying the gift in action, tools to discern what is the weaker side that needs strengthening, and spiritual disciplines to work on for each gift (1998:).[471]

Based on the criteria of lasting fruit ("the fruit will last"—John.15:16) and servanthood ("equipped to serve"—Ephesians 4:12) Wimber offers appropriate questions to help weigh expectations:

1. *Apostolic function*—How many disciples and churches are there as a fruit of your ministry?

2. *Prophetic function*—Do the prophetic words benefit others? How many believers are equipped to prophesy?

3. *Evangelistic function*—How many have been won and brought into the life of the church? How many evangelists have been trained and released?

4. *Pastoral function*—How many people have been equipped for life and ministry? How many are able to help others in the same way?

5. *Teaching function*—How biblically accurate, personally helpful, and culturally current is the teaching? How many teachers have been equipped and released?[472]

---

[469]Ibid., 255.
[470]Clinton and Clinton, *Unlocking Your Giftedness*, 1998.
[471]Ibid., 256-291.
[472]Wimber, 1997b, 12.

Gifts Tests

Most of the so-called "gift-tests" consist of questions about one's experience from ministry, as well as preferences and interests. Clinton points out that the results are only indicators, and that people's varying ego-strength will influence the results.[473] He resists using gift-tests in churches, where he rather thinks it is important to "get people into serving and stewardship . . . Let people drift towards their gifts".[474] When motivating a church for giftedness identification and development he thinks it is important to emphasize that the goal is not to give "people a new thing to do," but to "develop people, help them be good stewards of their gifts/abilities." He does not recommend assessing newcomer's and teenager's gifts but suggests rather focusing on their interests/abilities.

It is important to help people reflect on their destiny and to motivate them to be intentional about discovering and developing their gifts. Taking "the students" away from their everyday life, perhaps on a retreat, makes it easier for them to get a good perspective on their ministry. Clinton emphasizes how important it is "to raise awareness that there is more out there" through preaching and modeling, and suggests to "ask; 'are you satisfied?' and observe symptoms of it (stress, etc.)".[475]

Even if the issue at hand is to develop oneself or if it is to help others, Clinton's suggestions can be a good starting point:

1. Design training exercises,

2. Evaluate day-to-day experience, and

3. Become intentional; develop your own growth program, and get accountability![476]

Conclusion

These applications show that Wimber's dynamic model provides a solid and adequate methodological basis for the development of gifts. Compared to models that are more static, the gracelet-ministry-gifted equipper (office) model provides an excellent framework for development since

---

[473]Clinton, 1999.
[474]Ibid.
[475]Ibid.
[476]Ibid.

growth in frequency and effect is the core of the model. Based on Wimber's model, the various tools and models can facilitate the development from gracelets, into ministries, and into gifted equippers (offices).

5: LEVELS OF CHARISMATIC MINISTRY

Are "Gracelet," "Ministry," And "Gifted Equipper" Useful Labels?

In this chapter, I will evaluate Wimber's division between three levels of charismatic ministry and the labels he uses by comparing it with the Biblical material, mainly the Pauline letters, to see whether it captures the main concerns of the text. The intention is not to extract and develop Paul's own model, but simply to investigate whether Wimber's gracelet-ministry-gifted equipper (office) model has a solid basis in the Pauline writings and can account for the relevant material.

There are a few factors that can be used to argue for a division between different levels.

1. The fact that the grammar and variations between which gifts are mentioned in different forms in Paul's catalogues of spiritual gifts seems to indicate various levels or degrees of power/strength of many of the gifts.

2. There is another hint in 1 Corinthians 12:4–5: "different kinds of gifts. . . different kinds of service. . . different kinds of workings of power." Is it possible that Paul here refers to three different levels, namely development from gift (gracelet), to service (ministry), to workings of power (gifted equipper—office)?

3. Based on the assumption that the impartation of spiritual gifts is a fundamental part of equipping for ministry "to prepare [or equip] the people for works of service [or ministry]" (Ephesians 4:12) this might indicate a continuation and development from "spiritual gifts" to "ministries."

Grudem comments that Paul in "some cases names the specific gift . . .

154

and in other cases he names the persons who have those gifts".[477] He further distinguishes between persons with an "officially recognized gifted equipper (office) in the church (such as 'apostles' and 'pastor-teacher')," and named persons without official gifted equippers (offices). He writes that "in other cases, though the person is named, it is not necessary to think there was any official recognition or establishment in gifted equipper (office) in front of the entire church" (such as evangelists and prophets).[478] What is interesting about Grudem's model is the way he uses the grammar in the text to build his case. He defines the "unofficial persons" by showing how the gifts of encouragement, giving, and mercy are listed in Romans 12: "the one who encourages," the "one who contributes," and "he who does acts of mercy." Later in this chapter, I will try to categorize all the appearances of various gifts in a similar manner.

Spittler argues that some gifts can be "occasional," some are "continual and reside," some are "episodic and linger," some "become a lifestyle," and when a gift is "officially recognized" it becomes an "gifted equipper (office)".[479] He also draws a parallel to the Trinity. Spittler contrasts the different levels by making these comparisons and descriptions:

F9: Gracelets – Ministries – Gifted equipper (office), Adapted from Spittler, 1999.		
Level 1 – Gracelets	**Level 2 – Ministries**	**Level 3 – Gifted equipper (office)**
Gifts	Services	Activities
Extraordinary (Rare)	Occasional	Common
		Officially Recognized
	Episodic and Lingers	Continual and Reside
		Lifestyle

As mentioned above is it also possible that the three words Paul uses in 1 Corinthians 12:4–5; "different kinds of *charismatōn* (gifts) . . . *diakoniōn* (services). . . and *energematōn* (works of power)," can indicate three levels —gifts, services, and gifted equipper (office). The main reason why I am hesitant to argue strongly that this is the case is the fact that the word *diakonia* is used for serving and particularly for serving tables (Acts 6:2–3). It is linked to the particular gifted equipper (office) of deacon (Philippians

---

[477]Grudem, 1996, 1020.
[478]Ibid., 1020.
[479]Spittler, 1999.

1:1). It is therefore difficult to argue that it refers to a certain level of spiritual gifting (the ministry level). On the other hand is it not hard to argue that *charismata* can be meant to represent the first level—gracelets—and that *energemata* can represent the third level—gifted equipper (office)—since "works of power" is possibly linked to strong gifting. I will therefore conclude that it must be regarded as a possibility that Paul is referring to three levels of gifting, although I am hesitant to argue that this is the most likely interpretation.

ANALYSIS OF THE VARIOUS GIFT PASSAGES

Based on the indications listed above I will assume that Paul had a more or less established model of development in giftedness, and that it is not coincidental which *charisma* he mentions on the various levels. Since this is a thesis about Wimber, I will use his number of levels (3) as well as his labels (gracelets/ministry/gifted equipper). I propose that it is not coincidental which *charisma* Paul mentions on the gracelet level, which he mentions on the ministry level, and which he mentions on the gifted equipper (office) level. I will test the model by applying it to the material to see whether it can account for it, as well as analyze the results it can produce.

If we look at the major gift passages, we see that Paul mentions the various *charismata* in different grammatical forms. Based on Grounded Theory methodology I established three categories and grouped the grammatical forms in which the various *charismata* occur. The first I called "object," as "having a single prophecy to share," (not as "having a gift"), or as "administration." The second "does" like "prophesies," and the fourth "is" like "is a prophet." The proposal I will test is that the *charismata* occurring in these forms correspond with the three "levels" of gifting which Wimber called "gracelet," "ministry," and "gifted equipper (office)," as shown in the table above. The table below displays the link between the categories of grammatical forms with the three levels of *charismata* and gives one example of each.

F10: Categories, Levels, Illustration, and Examples			
Category	Level	Illustration	Example
Object	Gracelet	God gives administration	*Kybernēsis* (1 Corinthians 12:28)
Does	Ministry	Is teaching	*Didaskōn* (Romans 12:7)
Is	Gifted equipper (office)	Is a prophet	*Profētas* (1 Corinthians 12:28)

A few examples: The expression *didōtai…allō de profēteia* in 1 Corinthians 12:8 can literally be translated "given to another prophetic speech," which can indicate that it is only a momentary thing, a gracelet given for a specific time and purpose. The phrase *kybernēsis* in 1 Corinthians 12:28 can be translated with "administration-tasks," which treats the *charisma* as an object, and indicates that it is something, a gracelet, the person was given at the specific time. *Ho didaskōn* in Romans 12:7 literally means "the one who is teaching," which can indicate that this is something the person does with some regularity. *Prophētas* in 1 Corinthians 12:28 translates "prophets," which ties the *charisma* very closely to the person's identity, and thereby makes it likely that he or she is recognized as a "gifted equipper (office) holder."

The table below presents the codes I have used in the summary column of the next table to summarize the occurrence of the various grammatical forms.

F11: Coding of the Grammatical Forms		
G = gracelet, M = ministry, O = office		
Code	Definition	Category
G	Only gracelet	Object
G+M	Not gifted equipper (office), but both gracelet and ministry	Object+ <u>does</u>
M	Only ministry	<u>Does</u>
G+M+O	All three categories	Objec + <u>does</u> + **is**
O	Only gifted equipper (office)	**is**

This overview is limited to the Pauline texts. I have limited the selection of texts to the gift-taxonomies where *charisma* is used in a narrow sense referring to a particular manifestation of grace.[480] Although Wimber lists marriage and celibacy (1 Corinthians 7:7), I have chosen to not include this verse since these gifts are not included in any of the gift taxonomies. I have primarily based this study on the main gift-taxonomies, and secondly included other occurrences of the *charismata* which are found there in order to get more material to work on.

F12: Charismata appearing as only "gracelet" and charisma appearing as "gracelet, ministry, office"				
Charisma	**Gifts of Healings**	**Worship Leading**	**Prophecy**	**Teaching**
1 Cor 12:8-10	*charismata iamatōn*		*profēteia*	
1 Cor 12:28	*charismata iamatōn*		**profētas**	**didaskalus**
1 Cor 12:29-30	*iamatōn*		**profētai**	**didaskaloi**
1 Cor 13:1-3			*echō profētian*	*glossais tōn antrōpōn lalō*
1 Cor 13:08			*profēteiai*	
1 Cor 14:06			*profēteia*	*didachē*
1 Cor 14:26-27		*psalmon*		*didchēn*
Rom 12:6-8			*profēteian*	*didaskōn*
Eph 4:11			**profētas**	**didaskalus**
1 Thess 5:12-22			*profetēias*	
1 Pet 4:10-11				*lalei*
Summary	G	G	G + M + O	G + M + O

In the summary column of the table above we see that only two charismata, prophecy and teaching, occurs in all the three categories, and only two occur only as gracelet, worship leading and gifts of healings.

---

[480]See word study of *charisma* in Chapter 7.

F13: Charismata appearing as both "gracelet" and "ministry" but not as "office"								
Charisma	Word of wisdom	Word of knowledge	Discernings of spirits	Faith	Effects of miracles	Kinds of tongues	Interpret. of tongues	Revelation (vision)
1 Cor 12:4-7					ener-gēmatōn			fanerōis
1 Cor 12:8-10	sofias	gnōseōs	diakriseis pnevmaton	pistis	ener-gēmata dy-nameōn	genē glōssōn	hermēneia glōssōn	
1 Cor 12:28					dynameis	genē glōssōn		
1 Cor 12:29-30					dynameis	glōssais lalusin	diermēnev-usin	
1 Cor 13:1-3	eidō ta mystēria pante	Pasan ten gnōsin		echō pasan ten pistin		glōssais tōn an-gelōn lalō		
1 Cor 13:8		gnōsis				glōssai		
1 Cor 14:6		gnōsei				glōssais lalōn		apokalypsei
1 Cor 14:26-27						glōssan + glōssē tis lalei	hermenēian	apokalypsin
1 Thess 5:12-22			dokimadsete					
Heb 2:1-4					Sēmeiois dynamesin			
Summary	G + M	G + M	G + M	G + M	G + M	G + M	G + M	G + M

In the table above we see that eight charismata occur on the gracelet and ministry levels, but not on the office level: word of wisdom, word of knowledge, discernings of spirits, faith, effects of miracles, kinds of tongues, interpretation of tongues, interpretation (of dreams).

F14: Charismata appearing only as "ministry"								
Charisma	Administration	Exhortation	Giving	Helps	Mercy	Service	Ruling	Martyrdom
1 Cor 12:4-7						diakoniōn		
1 Cor 12:28	kybernēseis			antilēpseis				
1 Cor 13:1-3			psōmisō panta hyparkjonta					paradō to sōma
Rom 12:6-8		parakalōn	metadidus		eleōn	diakonian	proistamenos	
1 Thess 5:12-22		Nuthetuntas nutheteite + parakalumen + paramytheisthe						
1 Pet 4:10-11						diakonei		
Summary	M	M	M	M	M	M	M	M

159

In the table above we see that seven charismata occur only on the ministry level: administration, giving, exhortation, helps, mercy, ruling, martyrdom. We also see that only one gracelet, service, occurs only on the ministry and office-levels.

F15: Charisma appearing only as "office"			
Charisma	**Apostles**	**Evangelist**	**Pastor-teacher**
1 Cor 12:28	*apostolus*		
1 Cor 12:29-30	*apostoloi*		
Eph 4:11	*apostolus*	*evangelistas*	*poimenas (kai didaskalus)*
Summary	O	O	O

In the table above we see that three *charismata* occur only on the gifted equipper (office) level: apostle, evangelist, and pastor/shepherd.

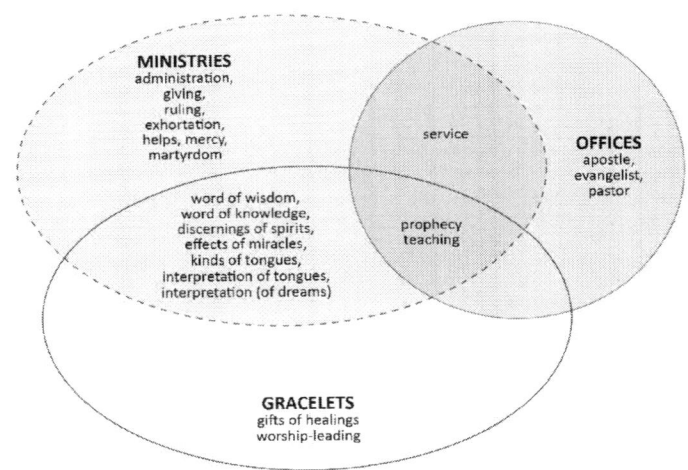

F16: Venn Diagram of Gracelets, Ministries, and Gifted equippers (offices)

The fact that none of the charismata occur only on the gracelet and gifted equipper (office) levels, the two sides of the spectrum, might indicate that this could be a useful way to organize the material.

I will now look closer at these findings and analyze the suggested pattern to determine whether it is meaningful. I will first look closer at the gracelet, ministry, and gifted equipper (office) levels to see which *charismata* are mentioned on each and ask why certain *charismata are* not mentioned on the gifted equipper (office) level.

GRACELETS

Paul mentions twelve *charismata* on the gracelet level. We see from the table above that inspired singing/worship leading (*psalmon* in 1 Corinthians 14:26–27)[481] and gifts of healing are the only two *charismata* mentioned only on the gracelet level and not on any other level. Eight other *charismata* are mentioned on the ministry level as well: word of wisdom, word of knowledge, discernings of spirits, faith, effects of miracles, kinds of tongues, interpretation of tongues, interpretation (of dreams). Two are mentioned on the gifted equipper (office) level as well: "prophecy" and "teaching."

The fact that there are hardly any *charismata* which are limited to the gracelet level suggests that the gifting should develop from sporadic gracelets to ministry, and partly to gifted equippers (offices).

MINISTRIES

Based on the word-study presented in Figure 16, we can see that there are seven *charismata* which Paul mentions only on the ministry level:

1. Administration,[482]

2. Giving,[483]

---

[481]See Dunn, 1975, 238 for a throughout analysis of *psalmon*.

[482]*Kybernesis* in 1 Corinthians 12:28.

[483]*Psomiso panta hyparkjonta* in 1 Corinthians 13:1-3 and *metadidus* in Romans 12:6-8.

3. Exhortation,[484]

4. Helps,[485]

5. Mercy,[486]

6. Ruling,[487] and

7. Martyrdom.[488]

Based on the characteristic of these *charismata* I would suggest that it would not make sense to mention them on the gracelet level, because the actions they refer to are not dependent on super-rational power/revelation as are the eight which we find on both the gracelet and ministry levels. I would therefore suggest that these *charismata* are what Wimber calls "role," a natural part of every Christian's life. Therefore, there is also an element of development represented although these *charismata* are mentioned only on the ministry level.

"Service"[489] is the only *charismata* which Paul mentions only on the ministry and gifted equipper (office) levels (as "deacon").

GIFTED EQUIPPERS (OFFICES)

It must be noted that it is in the pastoral letters we find most of the occurrences of *charismata* that are mentioned on the gifted equipper (office) level. As mentioned in Chapter 7, the origin of the pastoral letters has been debated. This may show a development in Paul's writings, but that does not basically change the argument in this chapter. This development from spontaneous exercising of *charismata* to more established gifted equippers (offices) and structures is a perfect example of how people's ministries can develop.

---

[484]*Parakalon* in Romans 12:6-8 and *nuthetuntas paramytheisthe nunteteite.*

[485]*Antilepseis* in 1 Corinthians 12:28.

[486]*Eleon* in Romans 12:6-8.

[487]*Proistamenos* in Romans 12:6-8.

[488]*Parado to soma* in 1 Corinthians 13:1-3.

[489]*Diankonion* in 1 Corinthians 12:4-7, *diakonian* Romans 12:6-8, and *diakonei* 1.Peter 4:10-11.

Gifted equippers (offices) Mentioned by Paul

Paul mentions five gifted equippers (offices). The three *charismata*, apostle, evangelist, and pastor (-teacher) are only mentioned as gifted equippers (offices). Evangelist (*evangelistas*) and pastor-teacher (*poimenas kai didaskalus*) are only mentioned in Ephesians 4, but apostle is also mentioned in 1 Corinthians 12:28 (*apostolus*), and in 1 Corinthians 12:29–30 (*apostoloi*).

Teaching and prophecy are the only two *charismata* which are mentioned on all the three levels. Teaching is mentioned on the gracelet level in 1 Corinthians 14:26–27,[490] and in 1 Peter 4:10–11. We find it as ministry in Romans 12:6–8,[491] 1 Corinthians 14:6,[492] and in 1 Corinthians 13:1–3.[493] As gifted equipper (office) it appears in 1 Corinthians 12:29–30.[494] Prophecy is mentioned on the gracelet level in 1 Corinthians 12:8–10[495] and in 13:8.[496] It appears as ministry in Romans 12:6–8,[497] 1 Corinthians 13:1–3,[498] and 14:6.[499] As gifted equipper (office), it appears in 1 Corinthians 12:29–30[500] and in Ephesians 4:11.[501]

Deacon is not mentioned on the gifted equipper (office) level in the texts I have included in this study but is found in Philippians 1:1.

Potential Gifted equippers (offices) not Mentioned by Paul

Paul never mentions the "healing" *charisma* on the gifted equipper (office) level. Is this a coincidence, or did Paul intentionally not mention some gifted equippers (offices) because he did not want to promote them? It is worth noting that almost all the gifted equippers (offices) Paul "leaves out" of his lists fall into two categories: some could obviously be dangerous as

---

[490]*Didchēn.*

[491]*Didaskōn.*

[492]*Didakje.*

[493]*Glossais tōn antrōpōn lalō.*

[494]*Didaskaloi.* Gee argues that "word of knowledge" is something more akin to inspired teaching (Gee 1930:27-34 and 110-19).

[495]*Profēteia.*

[496]*Profeteiai.*

[497]*Profēteian.*

[498]*Echō profēteian.*

[499]*Profēteia.*

[500]*Profētai.*

[501]*Profētas.*

gifted equippers (offices), and some functions should clearly be distributed among as many as possible.

These categories correspond clearly with a central part of Wimber's theology. Wagner describes Wimber's view like this: "He wanted to avoid the phenomenon of superstar healers and instead involve the whole Body in the ministry of healing".[502]

F17: Potential Gifted equippers (offices) not Mentioned by Paul		
Potential gifted equipper (office)	Based on charisma/gracelet	Why not?
Healer	Gifts of Healings	Danger
Miracle-worker/Magician	Miracles/Works of Power	Danger
Wise man/Oracle/Sage	Word of Wisdom	Danger
Sorcerer/Fortune-teller	Word of Knowledge	Danger
Discerner/Spiritual Expert	Discernment	Danger
Tongue Interpreter	Interpretation of Tongues	Danger
Helper	Helps/Aid	everybody should
Mercy	Mercy	everybody should
Exhorter	Exhortation	everybody should
Giver	Giving	everybody should
Tongue-speaker	Tongues	everybody should
Martyr	Martyrdom	very occasional
Strong Believer	Faith	specific/occasional
Worshiper	song (psalmon)	?

The dangers connected to the first group of potential gifted equippers (offices) are all connected to the status and function this person would get. Pride is never far away from a person given an exclusive function as for instance "spiritual expert," and the danger of hero-worshiping of the "magician" would be present. Most likely the goals of these potential gifted equippers (offices) would be better fulfilled if these functions were spread among many believers and less tied to particular persons holding recognized gifted equippers (offices).

The problem with the other group of potential gifted equippers (offices) is simply the limiting effect, which centralizing these functions into gifted equippers (offices) would have on these aspects of a congregation's life.

---

[502]Wimber, 1996, 39.

One recognized donor in a church is a good excuse for the others not to tithe. Much of the spontaneous function of prophetic messages in tongues would be lost if one person were the official tongue speaker or interpreter. Arguments for the fact that we all should exhort one another do not need to be listed.

Paul mentions one gifted equipper (office) which includes many of these potential dangers, the gifted equipper (office) as apostle, but these aspects of the apostolic function are not its central trust. Concerning the *charisma* of faith, clearly this is a function that cannot be turned on at will. It is faith in God and must be based on God's timing, since it is usually seen in connection with miracles and healings.

Some Charismata Mentioned only on the Gifted equipper (office) Level by Paul

Another interesting observation is the fact that three of the *charismata* Paul mentions on the gifted equipper (office) level do not have corresponding gracelets or ministries: evangelist, pastor, and apostle. I have earlier commented on the gifted equipper (office) of apostle's nature as consisting of several *charismata*, and I will look more closely at its exclusivity in the next chapter.

What are the implications for the definition of this gifted equipper (office) of the fact that there is no "evangelism" *charisma* mentioned by Paul on the gracelet or ministry level? Based on the assumption that all believers are called to witness, I will suggest that this is not something believers need extra inspiration or a *charisma* to do. The existence of gracelets or ministries of evangelism would (and do) give believers an excuse not to witness. Based on this, the gifted equipper (office) of evangelist should include a strong element of "equipping believers to witness."

Concerning the lack of gracelet or ministry called "pastor" the same logic can be applied; a central part of a pastor's ministry is to equip believers to pastor each other. Another possible explanation is the fact that the gifted equipper (office) of pastor by its very nature often consists of several *charismata*, e.g. exhortation, teaching, discernment, faith, ruling, or governments.

SUMMARY

The purpose of this chapter was to evaluate Wimber's gracelet-ministry-gifted equipper (office) model in terms of its ability to account for the relevant material in the Pauline writings.

I found that it is possible that the three labels Paul uses in 1 Corinthians 12:4-5, *charismata* (gifts), *diakonia* (services), and *energemata* (works of power) could indicate that Paul had a model of various levels of gifting. However, I do not find it likely that this refers directly to exactly three levels of gifting.

I investigated whether Wimber's division of three levels of charismatic ministry, as well as the labels he uses on these levels, has a solid basis in the Pauline writings. I made a double proposal to test Wimber's model. First, I proposed that it is not coincidental which *charismata* Paul mentions on which level. Secondly, the *charismata* occur in various forms that correspond with the three levels. Based on Grounded Theory methodology I grouped the grammatical occurrences in these four categories: "has," "object," "does," and "is."

The fact that none of the *charismata* occur only on the gracelet and gifted equipper (office) levels, the two sides of the spectrum, might indicate that this could be a useful way to organize the material.

The fact that there are hardly any *charismata* which are limited to the gracelet level, suggests that the gifting should develop from sporadic gracelets to ministry, and then partly to gifted equippers (offices).

6: WIMBER'S THEOLOGY IN CONTEXT

Wimber's Theology in the Context of Contemporary Theology

This chapter is not an attempt to give anything like a full presentation of other theologies of *charismata*. I have chosen not to do a systematic comparison of Wimber's model with the other models, but rather to look for common points and aspects that support or oppose Wimber's dynamic aspects.[503]

THE PERMANENT VIEW OF *CHARISMATA*

Something which has characterized Lutheran circles has been the passive attitude that "every Christian has received his gift, and it is important to use it".[504] Sigvart Riiser does not belong to this category, but he describes this view as surprisingly unworried by the lack of Biblical support and strikingly eager to avoid the Biblical material that does not fit into this model. He believes this is the reason why Lutheran preaching has become so poor in this area.

> When the grace-gifts are expected to automatically be in place due to the Christian life, . . . only a exhortation is needed . . . They obviously seem to believe that grace-gifts are something that automatically comes with the re-birth. Thereby they are also forced to hold that the children receive their grace-gifts already in the baptismal

---

[503]Some of the categories I have used to sort the other views are based on particular aspects which stand out in comparison with Wimber's model, and some are based on denominational grouping. The categories are not mutually exclusive, and the arguments have been sorted into categories based on their essence—not on the respective authors' theologies as a whole.

[504]My translation, Riiser, 1970, 64.

bath to re-birth.[505]

Grudem believes that "in most cases, it seems that the New Testament pictures a *permanent* possession of spiritual gifts".[506] He bases this primarily on the body metaphor in 1 Corinthians 12:12–26, but also on the "titles" some people have (1 Corinthians 12:29 and Ephesians 4:11), and 1 Corinthians 13:2 where Paul says, "If I have the gift of prophecy." He further argues that Paul must have assumed "that the church will know whether someone who has the gift of interpretation is present" since he gave the requirement for such to be present (1 Corinthians 14:28). Lastly, he lists 1 Corinthians 14:28 ("thinks that he is a prophet"), Romans 12:6 ("having gifts") and 1 Timothy 4:14 ("that is in you"), and concludes that:

> All of these verses point in the direction of a permanent, or at least abiding and continuing, possession of gifts . . . Therefore it seems that in general[507] the New Testament indicates that people have spiritual gifts given[508] to them and, once they have them, they are usually[509] able to continue to use[510] them over the course of their Christian life.[511]

This view is exemplified by the immediate link between task and equipping we see in this definition of spiritual gifts:

> The spiritual gifts are for the equipping of the work that the triune God gives each of us as his children by pure grace, so that we together can function as his congregation for the edification of the congregation and to God's honor. They have two main aspects, in an inseparable unity: the manifold tasks he places us in, within the

---

[505]My translation, Ibid., 64.

[506]Grudem, 1994, 1025.

[507]He lists "marriage," "celibacy," as non-permanent in their very nature, and "evangelism," prophecy," "healing," and "faith" as exceptions in some senses. Ibid.

[508]"Some particular gift may be given for a unique need or event", Ibid., 1026.

[509]"If a person neglects his or her gift, and perhaps grieves the Holy Spirit or falls into serious doctrinal or moral error . . . the gift may be withdrawn". Ibid.

[510]"Although it is the ordinarily the custom of the Holy Spirit to continue to empower the same gift or gifts in people over time, nonetheless, there is a continual willing and deciding of the Holy Spirit to do this or not, and he may for his own reasons withdraw a gift for a time, or cause it to be much stronger or much weaker than it was". Ibid.

[511]"1 Corinthians 13:8-13 . . . indicates that the present spiritual gifts which we have are only for this age and will be superseded by something far greater". Ibid.

congregation, and the equally manifold equipping-mercy he gives us in accordance with these tasks.[512]

Søvik and Skottene do not see the gift catalogues as exhaustive, and believe that the apostle-ministry ceased with the Twelve.[513] They, interestingly enough, clarify that they regard the most common way to sort the gifts as unbiblical, ordinary and extraordinary, permanent and free/spontaneous, as well as the combination of these categories.[514] They suggest a distinction between gifts of speech and gifts of action, based on 1 Peter 4:11, which is not so different from Wimber and Clinton's models. Another interesting parallel to note is the fact that Hagin sees the manifestation gifts as equipping for the ministry/task a person is called to.[515]

The emphasis on ownership of gifts, which is exemplified in the Willow Creek Community Church *Network Manual*, contrasts with Wimber's more dynamic and flexible model:

> Spiritual gifts are divine endowments. They are abilities God has given to us to make our unique contribution. Every believer has at least one spiritual gift . . . Do not confuse spiritual gifts with natural talents—natural talents are given at birth but spiritual gifts at spiritual birth.[516]

A different form of this permanent view is represented by Katie and Don Fortune, who focus on what they call "motivational gifts".[517] They treat seven of the gifts (servant, teacher, guide, giver, administrator, mercy, and prophet) as a special category of gifts which they believe "were built into us when God made us," and which were "visible from our childhood".[518] The only basis they provide is Proverbs 22:6 and Psalm 139:13–16.[519] I will not give this any further attention since it seems to have a very weak basis in the Pauline texts.

Ragnar Skottene opposes the charismatic belief that exercising of the nine extraordinary gifts should be a part of every normal and healthy

---

[512]My translation, Søvik and Skottene, 1983, 12-13.

[513]Ibid., 57.

[514]Ibid., 44-47.

[515]Hagin, 1975, 10-11.

[516]Bugbee et. al., 1994, 8.

[517]Katie and Don Fortune, *Discover your God-given Gifts*, 1987.

[518]Ibid., 4.

[519] Their other material is not readily available.

Christian's life. He does not write explicitly that everybody needs to stick with the gift they have received, but underlines the Spirit's work of "refreshing" old gifts.[520] Turner argues that this is a misunderstanding of Paul. He points to the fact that Paul, in 1 Corinthians 14:13, encourages those who have tongues to pray for interpretation.[521] He describes this view as portraying

> Paul as a fatalist in respect of the distribution of gifts, and the analogy of the body has been taken to mean that the nature of any particular believer's gifting will be as constant as the function of the bodily organs.[522]

THE SEMI-PERMANENT VIEW OF *CHARISMATA*

I found it necessary to make this in-between category to separate the following positions from the "permanent" category above. These authors are representative of conservative evangelicals responding to the charismatic challenge.

One example of a model which holds the permanent position, but attempts to account for the gifts that seem more sporadic, is the Norwegian book *You Shall Receive Power*, co-authored by several Lutheran charismatics. They distinguish between what they call "the manifestations of the Spirit" and "permanent services".[523] "Each of us . . . has . . . a [spiritual] gift . . . We have received our gift in and with our service in the congregation".[524] The authors view the gifts in 1 Corinthians 12:8–10 as the manifestations which the Spirit spontaneously gives again and again to various people.[525]

In "permanent services," they include all other gifts, and write that these are characterized by being tied more-or-less closely to specific persons, probably for life. They mention "apostle," teacher," and "evangelist" as examples.[526] They base this separation into two groups on which gifts

---

[520]Skottene, 1980, 78.

[521]Turner, 1998, 276.

[522]Ibid., 277.

[523]Hesselberg et. al., 1977, 136.

[524]Ibid., 139.

[525]Ibid., 135.

[526]Ibid., 137.

are mentioned, and which are not mentioned, in the gift catalogue in 1 Corinthians 8–10. They argue that the permanent services and the spontaneous manifestations should work together, because the list in 1 Corinthians 12.28 includes gifts from both categories.[527] The model has similarities to Wimber's distinguishing between the gracelets of Romans and Corinthians and the gifted equippers (offices) of Ephesians, but the noted problem with 1 Corinthians shows that these categories cannot be established by simply looking at which gifts are mentioned in the 1 Corinthians 12:8–10 list. I will come back to this below.

Jens Petter Jørgensen divides clearly between spontaneous gifts and permanent services. He calls some gifts permanent services and tasks in the congregation, and some "more spontaneous spiritual manifestations".[528] Word of Wisdom, Word of Knowledge, Tongues, and Interpretation of Tongues, are gifts he regards as more spontaneous and sporadic.

When commenting on the nature of the prophetic gift, Karl Olav Sadnes gives a great example of the relationship between gracelet, ministry, and gifted equipper (office); "Many shared prophetic messages. After a time they got a position as prophets because they regularly shared prophetic messages".[529] He further argues that the service/gift-lists do not draw a sharp line between services of more coincidental and time limited character and fixed services which were permanent, and which included a recognized leadership role in the congregation.

FOCUS ON PERMANENT MINISTRY

This point of view focuses on *charismata* as either empowerment for permanent ministry, or as the ministry or gifted equipper (office) itself. The Catholic scholar Hans Kung states:

> *Diakonia* is rooted in *charisma*, since every *diakonia* in the Church presupposes the call of God. *Charisma* leads to *diakonia* since every *charisma* in the Church only finds fulfillment in service. Where there is a real *charisma*, there will be responsible service for the

---

[527]Ibid., 138.
[528]Jens Petter Jørgensen, 1986, 51.
[529]My translation, Karl Olav Sadnes, 1996, 244.

edification and benefit of the community.[530]

Kung views the *diakonia* as the exercising of the *charisma*, and the *charisma* only as the empowering. It is also interesting to note that he defines even vocation/gifted equipper (office) as a manifestation, although this does not have a punctual meaning:[531]

> The permanent ministries in the community have the same characteristics as charisma, insomuch as in each case God calls a particular individual to a special ministry in the community and at the same time gives him the power to fulfill that ministry . . . Each vocation is a manifestation, individuation, and concretization of the one Charism of Jesus Christ.[532]

We can find this view in other schools as well. Surprisingly enough, Kenneth Hagin views spiritual gifts as something we need to function in the service/ministry God calls us to, even if it is only a serving gift like helps.[533]

This view links spiritual gifting closely to ministry. Lutheran ordination theology regards spiritual gifts as equal to ministry, holding that a spiritual gift is the ministry/task a person is doing, when he or she through ordination is equipped by God to do the task. This close link to ministry is also present in Engelsviken's definition of spiritual gifts as,

> the ministry/task and/or the equipping for ministry which the Holy Spirit by pure grace gives to each Christian so that he or she in word and deed can witness that "Jesus is Lord" so that the Christian church is built up.[534]

A chapter in Sandnes book *I Tidens Fylde* is titled "Spiritual gifts and ministries,"[535] but he does not share Wimber's perspective on gifts/gracelets and ministries as a part of a continuum. He partly uses ministry as a descriptive word for "non-charismatic gifts," and partly as a characteristic all spiritual gifts should have.

---

[530]Kung, 1967, 394.

[531]"No question of a vocation which comes and goes uncertainly, it remains constant and remains constant associated with specific persons". Ibid., 394.

[532]Ibid., 395.

[533]Cited by Bjørneset, 1986, 17 from Hagin, 1975, 10-11.

[534]My translation, Engelsviken, 1985, 65-66.

[535]Sandnes, *I Tidens Fylde*, 1996. My translation of "Nådegaver og Tjenester."

This view tends to focus on the non-charismatic gifts. Olav Skjevesland writes that "power-ministry is not everybody's business".[536] He bases this on the rhetorical question in 1 Corinthians 12:29f, where he assumes a negative answer.

THE CESSATIONIST VIEW OF *CHARISMATA*

Cessationism, as a theological framework, is somewhat distant from today's debate, but Spittler states: "until 20 years ago even Fuller taught cessation of the gifts, [they were] not needed." This was based on 1 Corinthians 13:10: "when perfection comes, the imperfect disappears." Perfection was understood to be at the closing of the canon,[537] or "when the church is mature," or "when the Gentiles are included in the church".[538] In the USA, this position was advocated by Benjamin B. Warfield, by the writers of the Scofield Reference Bible, and by Dallas Seminary. Jack Deere's *Surprised by the Power of the Spirit* is considered by many to be the definitive refutation of Warfield's cessationist doctrine. Deere, a former Dallas professor, changed his view after his interaction with the Vineyard movement and John Wimber.

Richard B. Gaffin Jr represents a contemporary cessationist viewpoint. He does not think that all gifts or all miracles have ceased, but "all revelatory or word gifts".[539] By "word gifts," he means prophecy, tongues/interpretation, word of wisdom, word of knowledge, and apostleship.[540] The fact that the New Testament canon is closed creates for him a tension with a "continuation of the prophetic gifts today" because it "relativizes the sufficiency and authority of Scripture".[541]

Since this view is not of direct relevance to this thesis, I will cut this presentation short by pointing to Turner's excellent critique in *The Holy Spirit and Spiritual Gifts*. He defines this position as relying on three kinds of argument:

(i) the New Testament itself anticipated the cessation of miraculous

---

[536]My translation, Skjevesland, in *Aarflot*, 1976, 28.

[537]Spittler, 1999.

[538]Grudem, 1994, 1036.

[539]Gaffin in Grudem, 1996, 42.

[540]Ibid., 42-45.

[541]Ibid., 44.

gifts; (ii) they in fact disappeared in church history, and (iii) there are no modern counterparts to the miraculous gifts of the New Testament.[542]

Throughout the rest of his book, he proves this position false.

THE EVANGELICAL CHARISMATIC VIEW OF *CHARISMATA*

Bobby and Richard Clinton are authors who have interacted with Wimber[543] and ended up with a related model of spiritual gifting. They divide the *charismata* into three categories: power gifts, word gifts, and love gifts, which correspond closely to Wimber's categories (power, discernment, speech, and service) except that they have combined power and discernment. The interesting aspect of the Clintons' model is the gifts they have chosen to place in the area where the circles overlap; healing, word of wisdom, (word of knowledge), (faith), and prophecy.

The following diagram displays the inter-play between overlapping categories.

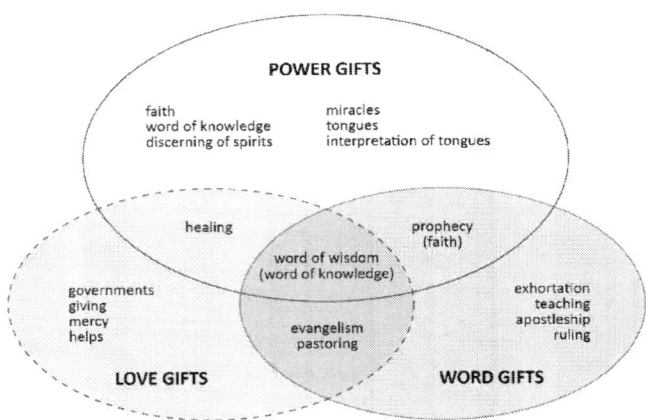

F18: Diagram of Power, Love and Word Gifts *(Clinton and Clinton, 1998, 126)*

---

[542]Turner, 1998, 286.

[543]Richard Clinton served as a pastor on Wimber's staff around 1990, and is currently pastoring a Vineyard church in Bern, Switzerland. Bobby Clinton is a professor of Leadership at Fuller Theological seminary in Pasadena, Los Angeles, USA.

The Clintons provide a model of the various levels of spiritual gifting which is closely related to Wimber. They divide between "vested" and "non-vested" gifts (compared to Wimber's gracelet, ministry, gifted equipper). "Vested" is defined as gifts "God releases through us, which we can control,[544] or more accurately:

> *Vested* gifts are gifts that appear repeatedly in a persons' ministry and can be repeated at will by the person. *Non-vested* gifts are spiritual gifts that appear situational and cannot be repeated at will by the person.[545]

The Clintons relate non-vested gifts primarily to the taxonomy in 1 Corinthians 12.8–10 and vested gifts mainly to the other taxonomies. Their third main aspect is their focus on the whole "giftedness set." By this, they mean a person's mix of natural abilities, acquired skills, and spiritual gifts.[546]

Earlier I commented on the difference between Wimber and Wagner's definitions of *charismata* and "role."[547] While Wagner's view has many similarities with Wimber's, it is less dynamic and more focused on finding one's gift. It seems like he mixes Wimber's dynamic view with a Pentecostal view of all gifts residing in one's spirit:

> He [Wimber] calls them "graces." Because you have the Holy Spirit, you have all the gifts and God lets you operate in the various gifts according to what is needed in the situation. I believe that each one of us has one or several gifts.[548]

Dennis and Rita Bennett state that the idea of "permanent ownership" is erroneous.[549] They argue that this "makes some the official interpreters, experts" and that this "leads to pride, stagnation, . . . [and] concentration

---

[544]Clinton, 1999.

[545]Clinton and Clinton, 1998, 130.

[546]See Ibid., Chapter 10, "What is the Goal of Development" and Figure B.1 in Appendix B concerning "the giftedness set," and Table B.1 in Appendix B concerning how the three aspects of the giftedness set are separated and interrelate {Are these appendices in the Clinton book? I assume so, therefore inserting "Ibid."}.

[547]"Feil! Bokmerke er ikke definert..Feil! Fant ikke referansekilden.Feil! Fant ikke referansekilden."

[548]My translation of Tangen, 1993, 28, citing Wagner.

[549]Dennis and Rita Bennett, 1980, 86.

around a few persons." They underline the dynamic aspect, but distance themselves from what they describe as the other extreme, namely "the idea that everybody has all the nine gifts of the Spirit which he can manifest/use whenever he likes to, a kind of a independent 'one-man-orchestra'".[550]

David Pytches' book *Spiritual Gifts in the Local Church* represents a pro-charismatic Anglican viewpoint. Turner, Dunn, Grudem, and Fee are scholars who more-or-less belong in this "charismatic evangelical" category. I found it useful to examine their viewpoints.

Lars Råmundal represents an Evangelical Covenant view. He serves as a bridge to the next category because he assigns the gifts to "born again" believers:

> A grace-gift is the Biblical name for the equipping the Holy Spirit by pure grace gives each born-again Christian so that she or he should be able to serve in the congregation, which is the body of Christ.[551]

Todd Hunter, once a Vineyard teacher, has made an interesting modification of Wimber's model.[552] He agrees with Wimber's dynamic aspect but has found it useful to divide between "primary gifts" and "situational gifts" (the revelatory gifts).

THE PENTECOSTAL VIEW OF *CHARISMATA*

The classical Pentecostal doctrine of the "special gifts of grace" would also limit the gifts to "born again" believers. Like Wimber, they regard the believer as a channel for the gifts to the congregation, but their starting point is somewhat different. They believe that all the gifts are in the spirit of the Spirit-filled believer.[553]

The classic Pentecostal position regards the nine gifts in 1 Corinthians 12 as the most important, and some as the only spiritual gifts. Donald Gee's *Concerning Spiritual Gifts* focuses only on these nine gifts.[554] Bloch-Hoell goes even further, and argues, that on the whole, the movement has favoured the sensational *charismata*, namely speaking with tongues, with or

---

[550]Ibid., 87.

[551]My translation, Lars Råmundal, 1997, 158.

[552] Todd Hunter is now an Episcopal Bishop.

[553]See the comments on Bonnke's view on page 26.

[554]Donald Gee, *Concerning Spiritual Gifts*, 1972.

without interpretation—which he describes as "not common in the early Movement"[555]—prophecy, and the gift of healing".[556] He describes the other gifts as "completely subordinate. They are referred to only because of the marked Biblicism within the movement".[557]

This view certainly has a strong dynamic element, but the fact that the "baptism in the Spirit," demonstrated by the use of the gift of tongues, is viewed as the entry gate into supernatural ministry,[558] strongly limits its flexibility. I have previously commented on Wimber's view on "baptism in the Spirit."[559]

Tongues as the initial sign of Baptism in the Spirit

The major difference between Wimber's theology of *charismata* and the Pentecostal tradition is how the *charisma* of tongues is viewed, whether it is the initial and mandatory sign of baptism in the Spirit or as a gracelet like the other gracelets. Hummel (not a Pentecostal) defines the classical Pentecostal doctrine and practice of the baptism in the Holy Spirit as a full reception of the Holy Spirit distinct from and subsequent to conversion, a second experience to be sought by all Christians. The initial physical evidence of the Spirit-baptism is speaking in tongues, and its result is power for witness and service through exercising the full range of spiritual gifts found in the New Testament. Pentecostals, he says, not only teach this doctrine, they experience it.[560]

Hummel argues that Paul and Luke do not use the phrase identically and has several text-interpretation arguments to support this.[561] Wimber holds that to "overwhelm is the fundamental character of the word *baptizō*".[562] This leads to his nuanced both/and view on this subject:

> Baptism is a flexible metaphor, not a technical term. Luke seems to regard it as synonymous with fullness (Acts 2:4, cf. 11–16). Therefore, so long as we recognize conversion as truly a baptism in the

---

[555]Bloch-Hoell, 1972, 145.

[556]Ibid., 142.

[557]Ibid., 151.

[558]Tegnander, 1991, 156.

[559]See Chapter 2, "A Sovereign Act."

[560]Hummel, 1979, 162.

[561] See also Jensen, *Touched by the Spirit*, 1975.

[562]Wimber, 1985c, 4.

Spirit, there is no reason why we cannot use baptism to refer to subsequent filling of the Spirit as well. This later experience, or experiences, should not be tied in with the tight second blessing schema, but should be seen as an actualization of what we have already received in the initial charismatic experience, which is conversion.[563]

It is important to point out that according to Bloch-Hoell, many Pentecostal teachers have distinguished between tongues as a *sign* (for all, based on Act.2:4), and tongues as a *gift* (not for all, based on 1 Corinthians 12:30). The early movement regarded *glossalia* "in connection with the Spirit Baptism . . . a permanent Gift of Grace".[564] Barratt distinguishes between "the ecstatic tongues which accompany the Spirit baptism and the gift itself, by which you can speak with tongues whenever you like and have the gift under control".[565] In this distinction between permanent and occasional gifts, we see a clear parallel to Wimber's distinction between gracelet and ministry.

The two Vineyard pastors, Rich Nathan and Ken Wilson, describe the "empowered evangelical view", which accepts the

reality to which Pentecostals and charismatics bear witness. That reality is simply this: there's more. Not a "Second Blessing," a baptism in the Spirit necessarily distinct from the new birth, necessarily signified by speaking in tongues; but a lifetime of subsequent and ongoing fillings of the Spirit.[566]

THE "FAITH" AND "DISCIPLESHIP" MOVEMENTS

The faith movement does not have a theology of *charismata* which is easily distinguishable from the Pentecostal camp.

Aril Edvardsen has a model of levels of spiritual gifting which is partly similar to that of Wimber. He writes that the Holy Spirit can work through us in two different ways: as a [sporadic] manifestation (1 Corinthians 12:7), or as more "permanent" service/ministry (1 Peter 4:10). When a person experiences that the Spirit works through him with a particular gift on

---

[563]Clark Pinnock in Spittler, 1976, 186 and in Wimber, 1985c, 4.

[564]Bloch-Hoell, 1972, 142.

[565]Barratt, 1972, 142.

[566]Nathan and Wilson, 1995, 212.

a regular basis, Edvardsen would say that the person has received the particular gift "in full portion".[567] This is very similar to the gracelet and ministry levels in Wimber's model, but he does not include the gifted equipper (office) level in his continuum. Edvardsen points out that "service/ministry" must not be confused with the service of deacon or the gifted equippers (offices) of apostle, prophet, teacher, evangelist, shepherd.

Derek Prince, representing the "Discipleship Movement",[568] defends the correctness of saying that a Christian has a spiritual gift if the Holy Spirit often manifests himself through a person with a particular *charisma*.[569] He bases this on Romans 12:6, 1 Corinthians 7:7 and 12:30. A more complete presentation and defense of this position can be found in Don Basham's *Tongues, Interpretation, and Prophecy*.[570]

Reinhart Bonnke advocates a more permanent view, where the "anointing" of the Holy Spirit is in focus, not specific *charismata*. Based on the way he describes Christian life and ministry it seems obvious that sporadic and spontaneous spiritual ministry, as Wimber calls "gracelets," is included in what Bonnke calls the "anointing." He equates the promised presence of Jesus (Matthew 28) with the Holy Spirit, and the Holy Spirit with His anointing, which he defines mainly as "power/strength" that can be activated by faith and trust, since it is God's power, which is constant. "When you are anointed, you are anointed for good".[571] Bonnke draws on the story of David, who did not run back to Samuel to get a new anointing when he faced Goliath. He concludes that one anointing is enough. One baptism is enough.

> We've got to learn to trust the anointing. If you feel that you are not anointed and need the anointing very much; appropriate the anointing by faith.[572]

This view is a good example of the Pentecostal understanding of the Holy

---

[567]Cited in Bjørneset 1986, 10 from Edvardsen, 1975, 174-175.

[568]"Discipleship Movement" is a broad description of neo-Pentecostal groups that articulate various forms of restorationist theology. For a description of the relationship between dispensationalism, cessationism and restorationism, see *Morphew, Breakthrough, Fifth Edition*, where a chapter is devoted to each of these.

[569]Prince in Bjørneset, 1986, 15.

[570]Don Basham, *Handbook on Tongues, Interpretation, and Prophecy*, 1971.

[571]Bonnke, 2001, 53.

[572]Ibid., 60.

Spirit's indwelling, or "anointing" the person, so that the *charismata* reside in the spirit of the believer. This view corresponds to Wimber's model by making all the gifts available to all believers (at least all who are "born again" or "anointed"). On the other hand, it differs by focusing on the permanency and availability of the "power" compared to the dynamic and flexible characteristic of Wimber's model. In Wimber's model, it is the Holy Spirit who plays the active role by putting the specific tool needed in the situation into the believer's toolbox, compared to the believer having a toolbox from where he can "appropriate" the tool he think he needs.

I commented earlier on the popular emphasis on the "Five-fold ministry" and restoration theology. A fundamental belief defining this "movement" is the idealization of the early church, and the need to re-establish the gifted equippers (offices) of Ephesians 4.

CONCLUDING COMMENTS

This limited review of contemporary theology shows that Wimber's model has touching points in various camps, but also meets critique and contradictory arguments. Hopefully, it has helped to put Wimber's view in relief.

As a final comparison, it is interesting to notice the modifications made by Todd Hunter. He agrees with Wimber's dynamic aspect, and believes "God can use any of the gifts through you when he wants".[573] However, he has found it useful to divide between "primary gifts" and "situational gifts." This is similar to Clinton and Clinton's distinction between vested and non/vested gifts. He uses his own teaching gift—which he regards as one of his primary gifts along with leadership—as an example. He says: "I am never wondering if it might come today" before he gets up to teach. In contrast, revelatory gifts are more situational for him. He does not have "the same confidence concerning revelatory gifts".[574]

---

[573]Hunter, 1999.
[574]Ibid.

7: JOHN WIMBER

A Portrait of John Wimber

Wimber was born in the Midwest in 1934, grew up in a totally unchurched family—four generations of unbelievers—and his alcoholic father left the family when he was a child. When he was twenty-one years old, he married Carol Kay Evans in Riverside, California.[575]

JAZZ MUSICIAN WRESTLING WITH THE HOLY SPIRIT

He worked several years in the entertainment-industry in Las Vegas as a jazz musician, and his group *The Righteous Brothers* often made the Top Ten. Larry L. Myers—a professional musician and later coworker—writes that: "John was an excellent musician. Having studied music from childhood, John had become not only a competent multi-instrumentalist [sax, guitar, and piano], but also a fine arranger and a successful record producer as well".[576] He had problems with drug abuse, and in 1962, he separated from his wife.[577]

Gunner Payne, a door-to-door evangelist and Bible study leader, lead Wimber to Christ in 1963. Carol, who came from a nominal Christian background, also gave her life to the Lord the same year. This gave them both "freedom from guilt and the fear of death, a purpose for living, and a renewed marriage".[578] They immediately started witnessing. Wimber relates, "for the first year of my Christian life I followed Gunner around, learning to do everything he did . . . I couldn't go to the market or a

---

[575]Wimber, 1999, 35.
[576]Myers, 1998, 17.
[577]Wright, 1996, 26.
[578]Wimber, 1992, 7.

hardware store without evangelizing someone".[579]

EVANGELIST AND PASTOR IN THE YORBA LINDA FRIENDS CHURCH

Wimber and his wife devoted the next six years to personal evangelism and gathered several hundred converts in Bible study groups. In 1970 he became a staff member of the church they had been members of for nine years—the Yorba Linda Friends Church—and started Biblical studies at Asuza Pacific University. He was very successful, but describes this period in *Power Healing* as "disquieting and confusing.[580] Although the Holy Spirit sometimes prompted him to evangelize and gave him supernatural knowledge, he was

> convinced that people who claimed these kinds of experiences were misled by the devil or suffered from psychological disorders. Natural means, rational and empirical, fitting into my Western worldview; anything that exceeded my ability to understand rationally was dangerous. Dreams and visions, I thought, were not compatible with sound doctrine.[581]

After Wimber had been a pastor for four years, he realized that something was wrong. He writes, "I loved the institution more than I loved the body of Christ".[582] He remembers how he had turned away people who had experienced the Holy Spirit or were addicted to drugs or homosexuality. He understood that he had hardened his heart towards the Holy Spirit.

CHURCH GROWTH CONSULTANT

He left the pastorate, and accepted the position as Founding Director at the Department of Church Growth at Charles E. Fuller Institute of Evangelism and Church Growth. He describes how, for "the next four years I introduced several thousand pastors to church growth principles, traveling

---

[579]Ibid., 83.
[580]Wimber, 1987, 23.
[581]Ibid., 25.
[582]Ibid., 28.

across America".[583] As an adjunct faculty member at the School of World Mission at Fuller Theological Seminary, he read George Eldon Ladd, and met Donald McGavran, Chuck Kraft, Paul Hiebert, Russel P. Spittler, and C. Peter Wagner, as well as many non-western pastors. He writes, "their courses and reports of signs and wonders from the Third World once again softened my heart toward the Holy Spirit and spiritual gifts".[584]

THE EMERGENCE OF THE VINEYARD CHRISTIAN FELLOWSHIP OF ANAHEIM

At this time, Wimber was struggling with his personal relationship with the Lord and had problems with overeating and high blood pressure. In addition, his son Chris turned away from the family and from God. During a trip to Detroit he broke down in despair, but God answered his prayer, waking him up in the middle of the night with Psalm 61 giving him a promise: "John, I've seen your ministry, and now I'm going to show you mine".[585]

At the same time, God showed his wife Carol through a vision that "he was going to do something that went outside of our denominational boundaries".[586] She received the gift of tongues, although she was strongly opposed to it, and stepped down from all leadership positions in the Quaker church they belonged to. She started attending a prayer meeting in a home with some other people from the church. She also read Ralph Martin's book *Hungry for God*,[587] which opened her up to the Holy Spirit's work. She relates: "John came once, but was not very impressed, because all they did was to pray and worship".[588] However, the Lord told him through Wagner to "Go home and start a church in Yorba Linda",[589] and confirmed it through other people. Wimber was therefore ready to become their pastor when the denomination asked the fast-growing group to leave. The Quaker church eventually gave them their blessing.

---

[583]Wimber, 1992, 84.

[584]Ibid., 85.

[585]Wimber, 1987, 34.

[586]Springer, 1987, 41.

[587]Ralph Martin, *Hungry for God*, 1974.

[588]Springer, 1987, 41.

[589]Wimber, 1987, 44.

MINISTRY IN THE MARKETPLACE

At the first meeting, May 8th 1977, 150 people came, and Wimber preached about how this Spirit-born church would carry "the reputation of illegitimacy that followed Jesus his whole life".[590] Wimber wanted them to look at the Scripture with new eyes. Springer recounts how Wimber "started teaching about healing, and we prayed for healing. But, nothing happened [for ten months] . . . culminating with a woman healed of flu when John prayed for her in February of 1978".[591] On the way home, he saw an open vision of honey dripping down on people from a huge honeycomb in the sky, and the Lord told him:

> It's my mercy, John. For some people it's a blessing, but for others it's a hindrance. There's plenty for everyone. Do not ever beg me for healing again. The problem is not on my end, John. It's down there.[592]

In April it finally started breaking loose. The Holy Spirit came powerfully at a home Bible study, and eventually in the Sunday service when Wimber released healing ministry to all who wanted it. He wrestled a while with the strange manifestations (falling and shaking), but the young people in the church took the power out on the streets. He "baptized hundreds of new converts during the next few months, in our pool and pools around town".[593]

LEAVING CALVARY CHAPEL AND BECOMING "VINEYARD"

The church became connected to the Calvary Chapel movement, and was called the Calvary Chapel of Yorba Linda. However, in May 1982 Chuck Smith—the founder and leader of the Calvary movement—asked them to leave. To what extent he gave his blessing to Wimber leaving the movement is not clear. Jackson writes:

> It was suggested that Wimber's church align with the Vineyard

---

[590]Springer, 1987, 41.
[591]Ibid., 42.
[592]Wimber, 1987, 52.
[593]Springer, 1987, 46.

churches . . . Chuck later told Kenn [Gulliksen] that he just assumed that the Vineyards would continue as a part of the movement but with a different flavor.[594]

Gulliksen had planted the first Vineyard church in LA in 1974. It started with two Bible studies, one in Larry Norman's and one in Chuck Girard's house, and attracted people like Keith Green, Bob Dylan, Debby Boone, and Hal Lindsey.[595] Their first public service was held at the Beverly Hills Woman's Club, but "they grew rapidly and began moving around from location to location, . . . at one point, they met for one year on the beach in Santa Monica at Lifeguard Station #15".[596] In addition, Brent Rue, Jack Little, John Odean, and Bill Dwyer had planted Vineyard churches, but the group were considered a part of the Calvary movement, only more charismatic.

Among those who changed their affiliation, along with Wimber, were Tom Stipe and John McClure. Ken Gulliksen willingly turned the leadership of the movement over to Wimber, and soon after that God gave Wimber a vision to plant 10,000 churches throughout America. From these it would also spread to England and throughout the world. The church met for many years in high schools and in a large warehouse in Anaheim. In 1991 they bought a larger commercial building on the border of Anaheim and Yorba Linda.

THE KANSAS PROPHETS, THE TORONTO RENEWAL, AND BATTLE WITH CANCER

In 1987, the movement was in a "desperate condition," and Mike Bickle—pastor of Metro Christian Fellowship in Kansas City—"offered encouragement and advice".[597] At the same time Paul Cain was instrumental in the salvation of Wimber's son Chris. Bickle's church joined the Vineyard, and Wimber allowed the "Kansas City Prophets" to minister to his church and to the movement. He also brought Cain along to conferences to promote his ministry, but after controversy was aroused, Wimber distanced himself

---

[594]Jackson, 1999, 86.
[595]Ibid., 82.
[596]Ibid., 80.
[597]Wright, 1996, 27.

from them in 1991.

What became known as the "Toronto renewal," broke out almost simultaneously in Anaheim and Toronto in January 1994, but the Airport Vineyard Christian Fellowship became the world-known renewal center. Wimber had to cope with a lot of criticism for many of the Toronto church's practices. Since, in his view, they did not receive the leadership and corrections the AVC board offered them, Wimber and the AVC board finally asked them to dissociate themselves from the AVC in December 1994.

In 1995 Wimber retired from the pastorate of Anaheim VCF—which then had about 6000 members—but had to take over again for a short period after Carl Tuttle resigned from the senior pastor position. Wimber fought with cancer the last few years of his life and died of it on November 17th1997. Shortly after that, his son Chris also died of cancer.

THE MAJOR THEMES IN JOHN WIMBER'S MINISTRY

Wimber's overarching meta-theme was the presence of the Kingdom of God. Four central themes emerge from that: healing/prophecy, renewal/church planting, compassion, and worship.

The Kingdom of God: Healing and Prophecy

Large portions of the story of how Wimber started the Anaheim Vineyard Christian Fellowship are closely connected with his perception of the work of the Holy Spirit. Shortly after his conversion, Wimber had an early experience with the Holy Spirit's power. Their young son was playing in the neighborhood and was stung by a swarm of bees. Wimber spontaneously prayed for healing and felt power go through his hands like electricity. All the blisters disappeared immediately. However, since he was taught that the spiritual gifts like healing had ceased with the apostles, he suppressed this experience for many years.

One of the people who probably influenced Wimber the most toward the healing ministry was the Catholic scholar Francis McNutt, whom he often used as a reference. Wimber and the Vineyard movement were, for a period, greatly influenced by the Kansas City prophets. These two themes are integrated in Wimber's healing model, called the "Five step model",[598] where prophecy as "word of knowledge" plays a crucial part in initiating healing.

The Kingdom of God: Renewal and Church Planting

While working at the Institute of Church Growth and Evangelism, Wimber attended a funeral that made a profound impact on him. A church that had planted fifty-six other churches and felt they had completed their mission, was symbolically buried by 20,000 people from its daughter-churches. He prayed: "Lord, if you ever call me to minister in another church, I promise it will be a sending church".[599] Wimber's goal was not to build a mega-church, nor was his focus to gather the masses to his church. Once he tried radio broadcasting, only to soon discover that it was not his call.[600]

Wimber has been accused of stealing members from other churches through his renewal conferences. Paul Hiebert and J. R. Coggins wrote, for instance, about a pastor in British Columbia who felt betrayed after pro-moting a "nondenominational" renewal conference hosted by Vineyard representatives, because they "started setting up Vineyard churches in the area and attracting those who had been blessed by the seminars".[601]

To counterbalance these claims, I would emphasize Wimber's willing-ness to give everything away and his efforts to bring renewal to all kinds of churches. He also put a ten year moratorium on church planting in the countries where he worked with the established churches, like "in UK, . . . [and] countries where he was invited through the connections of David Watson's Anglican friends".[602]

Anecdotally it has been said that when people/leaders from other churches approached him and wanted to become a part of the Vineyard, he used to tell them three times to "take the renewal home to their own church!" If they came back again in tears after the third attempt because they had been kicked out of their church, he would accept them.

Wimber's leadership philosophy matched his flexible and dynamic

---

[598]Wimber and Springer, 1987, 224.
[599]Nicholson, 1998, 18.
[600]Nerheim, 1992.
[601]Paul Hiebert and J. R. Coggins, 1989, 7.
[602]Nicholson, 1998, 19.

view of the spiritual gifts, as exemplified in the following criteria:

1. It is sometimes demonstrated by recognizing who is leading in a given situation.

2. It can never be assumed. It is only authenticated by a following.

3. It is tested: By continuing to demonstrate that you are a leader.[603]

The Kingdom of God: Compassion for the Poor and the Broken

Wimber called mercy and grace "our heritage," because "the sin-filled, hurting, and needy . . . [are] people just like us".[604] His compassion for the poor was demonstrated through theextensive benevolence ministry he started at the Anaheim Vineyard—free lunch and groceries for the poor every Sunday, and a large warehouse distributing food, clothes, and supplies for house-building teams. The low-stress, no-requirements, no dress code, come-as-you-are mentality opened the church for people from all classes. Wimber's theology of compassion is presented in *The Gospel to the Poor*, probably his least known book, published as a part of the Oasis Bible Study series.[605]

His compassion for the broken was also evident in the church's various specialist inner-healing ministries and the high priority given to recovery groups. The Anaheim Vineyard initiated one of the most successful healing ministries, led by Andy Comiskey. "Desert Stream Ministries" ministers healing to the sexually and relationally broken. Earlier Andy had his own struggles with the homosexual lifestyle.[606]

The Kingdom of God: Intimate Worship

A key Bible verse in Wimber's theology of worship is John 4:23: "the true worshipers will worship the Father in Spirit and Truth." He believed that worship is the church's primary calling and dedicated the first half-hour of the service purely to singing worship songs. He believed that worship should be directed toward God, intimately and personally, rather than to

---

[603]Wimber, 1995, 7. For a more extensive articulation on his philosophy of leadership, see Morphew, *John Wimber Pastoral Letters*.

[604]Wimber, 1996, 23.

[605]Wimber, *The Gospel to the Poor*, 1994.

[606]Andy Comiskey, 1989, "Introduction".

singing about God, being entertaining, manipulative/hyping, or used to warm up people before the sermon.

Wimber also wanted the worship style to be culturally relevant. Myers explains, "he had a personal, working knowledge of the contemporary pop/rock music scene, so that the music he liked, that he wrote, that expressed his heart, was the same musical idiom that most baby-boomers related to".[607] He wrote many widely used songs like "Spirit Song," "Isn't He," "I believe," and "Arms of Love." In 1978 Wimber established Mercy/Vineyard Publishing[608] to promote and distribute his music, which was later incorporated into Vineyard Music Group.

ANALYSIS OF JOHN WIMBER'S CONTRIBUTION TO THE CHURCH

Wimber's impact reached far into both evangelical and Pentecostal circles. His books have been translated into a dozen languages and sold millions of copies. His renewal conferences in the US, England, and South Africa were widely attended and impacted numerous churches and denominations.

Word: Expository Bible Teaching

Rich Nathan contrasts Wimber's ministry to revivals where expository teaching was neglected and subsequently died out. He states that,

> Better and more lasting results can be expected from John's ministry because it was always undergirded by teaching the eternal Word of God . . . people received not only an experience, . . . but a true message from the Scriptures.[609]

Many came to his seminars and workshops to experience the "ministry time," but nobody saw him pray for healing without first opening the Bible to teach.[610]

Compared to evangelicals and Pentecostals, who mainly drew their theology and teaching respectively from the letters of Paul and Acts, Wimber

---

[607]Myers, 1998, 16.
[608]Bogart, 1998, 23.
[609]Nathan, 1998, 20.
[610]Ibid.

focuses on the gospels. He saw the ministry of Jesus as an example of how we ought to do the works of Jesus today. Texts like Matthew 9:35–38 and Luke 4:18–19 held a central place in his theology and teaching.

Wimber's theology was largely based on Ladd's theology of the kingdom of God.[611] Don Williams writes, "Wimber rightly saw the center of Jesus' good news as the in-breaking of the Kingdom of God."[612] For Wimber the foundational premise, "is that the Kingdom of God has come in Christ, and that every Christian is called to preach and demonstrate the kingdom today".[613] Mark 1:15 was a central verse for him: "The Kingdom of God is near. Repent and believe the good news!"

E. E. Wright criticizes the Vineyard for "eroding Biblical authority and sufficiency . . . They have reversed the classic order in which Scripture produces, interprets and controls experiences".[614] He has also been accused of promoting extrabiblical practices. However, that criticism came from cessationist, who could not accommodate the contemporary use of spiritual gifts like prophecy. Wimber stressed the importance of testing all prophecies and manifestations on the Bible, and his foundation was solid: "none of these instructions will benefit if you neglect the fundamental principles of obedience to God's word and reliance on his compassion and mercy".[615]

Wimber and his theology were subject to much criticism because of his association with Paul Cain and later, the "Toronto renewal," which is beyond the scope of this thesis.

World: Power Evangelism

Wimber's first book, *Power Evangelism*[616] was already considered a classic when the second edition came out in 1992, having been translated into a dozen languages.[617] It opened the mystical world of signs and wonders for hundreds of thousands of Christians, providing a solid biblical basis and

---

[611]George Ladd, *A Theology of the New Testament,* 1974a, 410, 557, and *The Presence of the Future,* 1974b, 105-217.

[612]Don Williams, 1998, 14.

[613]Wimber, 1997a, 17.

[614]Wright, 1996, 64.

[615]Wimber, 1987, 55.

[616]Wimber, *Power Evangelism,* 1992.

[617]The original version came out in 1985 and was largely based on the MC510 course Wimber taught as an adjunct professor for Wagner in the early 1980's. Wimber, 1992.

practical guide to power encounters, divine appointments, and how to hear God's voice. Wimber had a deep commitment to equip the people of God to do the works of the Kingdom, to use the gifts of the Holy Spirit, and to expect power, not primary in the "charismatic prayer meetings" but in everyday life.

"Servant Evangelism" also become a popular concept in the Vineyard movement, largely because of Steve Sjogren's book, *Conspiracy of Kindness*.[618] Servant evangelism is about demonstrating God's love through outreaches based on acts of humble service (like toilet cleaning and house remodeling) and loving help (like free gift-wrapping, car washes, and soda-give-away on warm days). This is a "No guilt, no stress, low-risk and high grace"[619] approach to evangelism for shy Christians who do not enjoy street-corner-preaching. Sjogren writes about Wimber that he "didn't lose track of his un-churched roots. He never forgot the pain and frustration and meaningless existence that those outside of Christ face daily".[620]

Church: Organic Unity

In terms of church and denominational history, the Vineyard is normally placed in what has been called "the Third Wave." Wagner introduced this term, referring to the third outpouring of the Holy Spirit in the 20th Century. David Barrett estimated, in 1995, that 75 million believers worldwide belonged to the "mainline Third Wave" category.[621] With an emphasis on "signs and wonders," the

"the distinctive teachings of the Third Wave center around:

(1) a new perspective on what is called 'worldviews',

(2) the presence of the future, or the ministry of God's kingdom, in the present age, not just in a future-only kingdom, and

(3) 'power evangelism,' evangelism accompanied by dramatic manifestations of miraculous healings and prophetic utterances."[622]

Winson Synan describes Third Wavers as "mainline evangelicals who

---

[618]Steve Sjogren, *Conspiracy of Kindness*, 1993.
[619]Ibid., 1.
[620]Ibid., 22.
[621]Barrett, 1995.
[622]Armstrong, 1992, 62.

exercise the spiritual gifts and exercise signs and wonders, but who do not identify with either the Pentecostal or charismatic movements".[623] He traces the roots of this movement back to about 1980, and thinks that "This tendency may have started in California, in John Wimber's class at Fuller Theological Seminary."

Wimber's conception of the unity of the church was relational and organic. In his book *Beyond Intolerance*, he states: "we are one body, but we are in different organizational structures",[624] and argues that we should be able to experience a degree of unity with believers who, for instance, have a different view on baptism. He believed striving for total theological or practical agreement was based on the false assumption that unity must be organizational.

Don Lewis, Professor at Regent College, who attended a Wimber seminar, thought that "Wimber had a love-hate relationship with the church . . . and sensed a strong us-them mentality".[625] This may be accurate to a degree, but it was because of Wimber's strong love for the whole church that he criticized its practical cessationism, unbelief and "cold and lifeless orthodoxy".[626] He also spent a lot of his time traveling across the world to conduct renewal conferences, mainly for the non-charismatic evangelicals.

The post-Wimber worship style has also had its critics. "Their manner of worship generates a powerful atmosphere of emotion through repetitive choruses with weak content sung to a loud and fast beat. The congregation becomes an instrument played by the leader".[627] Despite this rather arbitrary statement, large portions of the evangelical Christianity have followed what Chuck Smith Jr. calls "Wimber's innovation . . . to use a band for worship",[628] not only for evangelism, like Calvary Chapel did. This was demonstrated by the many songs and CDs produced by Vineyard Music Group, and by how widely they have been used.[629]

Wimber said Vineyard churches should be based on relationships and maintained in home fellowships. He intended the home groups to be the primary entrance to the church, which were "side-door-based" in contrast

---

[623]Synan, 1997, 285.

[624]Wimber, 1996, 44.

[625]Cited in Wright, 1996, 64.

[626]Hiebert and Coggins, 1989, 8.

[627]Wright, 1996, 68.

[628]Smith, 1998, 17.

[629]Bogart, 1998, 23.

to attracting people to the front door through advertisements. He emphasized training of all the members as ministers and inspiring them to make connections with unsaved people through friendship evangelism and servant evangelism. He wanted the Sunday service to be a celebration for the Kingdom work the Lord had allowed the church members to partake in during the week. His model of a Sunday morning church service consisted of three parts: intimate worship, expository bible teaching, and "ministry-time." He saw participation in a home fellowship as the primary means of membership. Many Vineyard churches still do not practice formal membership.

Wimber's primary focus was the "equipping of the saints." Alexander Venter writes that this was what Wimber wanted to be remembered for. These were are written on his gravestone: "He equipped the saints".[630] In his view, the local church exists to be a training center for ministry in the world. It cannot therefore be stage or clergy centered. He emphasized "the priesthood of all believers," and the importance of releasing the ministry to all the believers. His understanding of the church was summarized in four metaphors, representing various aspects church life: family, hospital, school, and army.

---

[630]Venter, 2000, 172.

BIBLIOGRAPHY

PART ONE

Ashley, Timothy R. *The Book of Number, The New International Commentary,* Grand Rapids: Eerdmans, 1993.

Chase, Bishop Frederick. *Confirmation and the Apostolic Age,* London: MacMillan and Co, 1909.

Cho, Youngmo. *Spirit and Kingdom in the Writings of Luke and Paul,* Eugene: Wipf and Stock, 2005.

Erickson, Doug. *Living the Future: The Kingdom of God and the Holy Spirit in the Vineyard Movement,* Douglas Erickson Publication, Amazon CreateSpace, 2016.

Davids, Peter. *The Ministry of the Kingdom, Part 2,* unpublished manuscript that was part of the Vineyard Bible Institute curriculum.

Dunn, James *Baptism in the Holy Spirit: A Re-examination of the New Testament on the Gift of the Spirit,* Westminster: John Knox Press, 1977.
Jesus and the Spirit: A Study of the Religious and Charismatic Experience of Jesus and the First Christians as Reflected in the New Testament, London: SCM, 1975.

Ervin, Howard M. *These Are Not Drunken as Ye Suppose,* Plainfield: Logos International, 1968.
Conversion-Initiation and the Baptism of the Holy Spirit, Peabody: Hendrickson Publishers, 1984.

Holdcroft, L. Thomas. *The Holy Spirit, A Pentecostal Interpretation,* Springfield: Gospel Publishing House, 1979.

Hyatt, Eddie L. *2000 Years of Charismatic Phenomena, A 21st Century Look at Church History from a Pentecostal/Charismatic*

Perspective, Lake Mary: Charisma House, 2000.

Keener, Craig. *Gift and Giver, the Holy Spirit for Today*, Baker Academic, 2001.
Acts, An Exegetical Commentary, Four Volumes, Grand Rapids: Baker, 2012.
Miracles: The Credibility of the New Testament Accounts, 2 Volumes, Grand Rapids: Baker, 2011.
Spirit Hermeneutics: Reading Scripture in the Light of Pentecost, Grand Rapids: Eerdmans, 2016.

Kelly, J. N. D. *Early Christian Doctrines*, London: Adam & Charles Black, 1968.

Lyons, Thomas. *Revisiting The Riddle In Samaria: A Social-Scientific Investigation Of Spirit Reception In Luke-Acts In Historical Perspective*, 2020, Doctoral Dissertation submitted to Asbury Theological Seminar, February 2020.

Macchia, Frank D. *Baptized in the Spirit: A Global Pentecostal Theology*, Grand Rapids: Zondervan, 2006.

Kilian McDonnell and George T. Montague. *Christian Initiation and Baptism in the Holy Spirit: Evidence from the First Eight Centuries*, Collegeville: The Liturgical Press, 1991.

Menzies, Robert P. *Empowered for Witness: The Spirit in Luke-Acts*, Sheffield: Sheffield Academic Press, 1994.

Morphew, Derek. *The Mission of the Kingdom, the Theology of Luke-Acts*, Cape Town: Vineyard International Publishing, 2011.
Biblical Interpretation 101, Historic Rules for Reading the Bible, Cape Town, Vineyard International Publishing, 2012.
Breakthrough: Discovery the Kingdom, Fifth Edition, Cape Town, Vineyard International Publishing, 2019.
Demonstrating the Kingdom: Tools for Christian Disciples, Cape Town, Vineyard International Publishing, 2019.
The Kingdom Reformation: Rediscover Jesus: Review Everything! Cape Town: Vineyard International Publishing, 2020.

Nathan, Rich and Ken Wilson. *Empowered Evangelicals: Bringing Together the Best of the Evangelical and Charismatic Worlds*, Ann Arbor:

Vine Books, 1995.

Plummer, Alfred. *The Gospel According to St Luke, International Critical Commentary,* Edinburgh: T & T Clark, 1910.

Riggs, Ralph M. *The Spirit Himself,* Springfield: Gospel Publishing House, 1968.

Rhoads, David, Joanna Dewey, Donald Michie. *Mark as Story: An Introduction to the Narrative of a Gospel,* Fortress, 2012.

Turner, Max. *Power from on High: The Spirit in Israel's Restoration and Witness in Luke-Acts,* Sheffield: Sheffield Academic Press, 1996.

New Bible Commentary, editors D. Guthrie, J. A. Motyer, A. M. Stibbs, D. J. Wiseman. IVP, 1970.

NIDNTT, abbreviation for Colin Brown, editor. *New International Dictionary of New Testament Theology,* 3 *Volumes,* Exeter: Paternoster, 1975.

Ponsonby, Simon. *More,* Eastbourne: Kingsway, 2009.

Stott, John. *Baptism and Fullness: The Work of the Holy Spirit Today,* Downers Grove, IVP, 2006.

Stronstad, Roger. *The Charismatic Theology of St. Luke: Trajectories from the Old Testament to Luke-Acts,* Grand Rapids, Baker, 2012.

Wimber, John. *Power Healing,* London: Hodder and Stoughton, 1993.
Power Evangelism, London: Hodder and Stoughton, 1986.
Power Points, New York: Harper Collins, 1991.
Baptism in the Spirit, Audio Resource available from Wimber.org, 1991.
Equipping the Saints, The Gift of Prophecy, Vineyard Ministries International.

Young, E. J. *My Servants the Prophets,* Grand Rapids: Eerdmans, 1965.

PART TWO

Armstrong, John H.

1992   "In Search of Spiritual Power." In Horton, Michael Scott, ed. *Power Religion: The Selling Out of the Evangelical Church?*, Chicago, IL: Moody. 61–88.

Association of Vineyard Churches

1995   *Theological and Philosophical Statements.* Anaheim, CA: Association of Vineyard Churches

Austad, Torleiv

1989   *Bønn til Gud: fra Troens og Teologiens Liverse* Oslo: Credo

Barratt, T. B.

1908   "T. B. Barratt's Journals from 1906–1910." The property of Mrs. Solveig Barratt Lange. Oslo, Norway: Unprinted.

Barrett, David

1995   *The World Christian Encyclopedia.* New York, NY: Oxford

Basham, Don

1971   *Handbook on Tongues, Interpretation and Prophecy.* Monroeville, PA: Whitaker

Bauer, Walter

1979   *A Greek-English Lexicon of the New Testament and Other Early Christian Literature.* Chicago, IL: University of Chicago

Bennett, Dennis and Rita

1971   *The Holy Spirit and You: a Study Guide to the Spirit-filled Life,* London: Coverdale

1980   *Den Hellige Ånd og Du: En Studieveiledning til et Åndsfylt Kristenliverse* Oslo: Filadelfiaforlaget

Bittlinger, Arnold
1967   *Gifts and Graces. A Commentary on 1 Corinthians 12–14.*
          Translation from German by Herbert Klassen and Michael
          Harper. Grand Rapids MI: Eerdmans

Bjørneset, Ola Kåre
1986   *Bibelteologisk Vurdering av Nådegavebegrepet i ein del
          Nyere Karismatisk Populærlitteratur,* Unpublished Master
          thesis, Oslo: The Norwegian Lutheran School of Theology

Bloch-Hoell, Nils
1972   *The Pentecostal Movement. Origin, Development, and Dis-
          tinctive Character.* Oslo, Norway: Universitetsforlaget

Bonnke, Reinhart
2001   "Trust the Anointing." CD-recording from sermon held at
          "Camp Meeting 2001" at Oslo Kristne Senter. Kjeller, Nor-
          way: OKS

Bugbee, Bruce, Cousins, Don and Hybels, Bill
1994   *Network Manual.* From Willow Creek Community Church,
          Grand Rapids, MI: Zondervan.

Cannistraci, David
1996   *The Gift of Apostle.* Ventura, CA: Regal Books

Carson, D. A.
1992   "The Purpose of Signs and Wonders in the New Testa-
          ment." In Horton, Michael Scott, ed. *Power Religion: The
          Selling Out of the Evangelical Church?* Chicago, IL: Moody.
          89–118.

Carter, Howard
1946   *The Gifts of the Spirit.* Mineapolis, MN

Charmaz, Kathy
1994   "The Grounded Theory Method: An Explication and Inter-
          pretation." In Glaser, Barney G., editor. *More Grounded*

Theory Methodology: A Reader. Mill Valley, CA: Sociology Press. 95–116

Clinton, Richard W. and Clinton, Robert J.
1993   *Developing Leadership Giftedness: What leaders Need to Know About Spiritual Gifts to Develop Themselves and Their People. A self-study Manual.* Altadena, CA: Barnabas
1998   *Unlocking Your Giftedness.* Altadena, CA: Barnabas

Clinton, Richard W.
1999   "ML 521. Developing Giftedness in Leaders." Master level course at Fuller Theological Seminary, Pasadena, CA
2000   "Spiritual Gifts." Tape-recording of seminar held at the Norwegian Vineyard New Year Camp in Hurdal, December 30th. Oslo: Oslo Vineyard

Clinton Robert J.
1985   *Spiritual Gifts.* Alberta, Canada: Horizon House
1984   *Leadership Training Models.* Altadena, CA: Barnabas

Dunn, James D. G.
1975   *Jesus and the Spirit, a Study of the Religious Experience of Jesus and the First Christians as Reflected in the New Testament.* Philadelphia: Westminster
1990   *Unity and Diversity in the New Testament, An Inquiry into the Character of Earliest Christianity,* London: SCM Press

Engelsviken, Tormod
1985   *Tent for å Tjene. Nådegavene og Tjenestene i Menigheten.* Oslo: Norsk Luthersk Forlag

Fee, Gordon D.
1987   *The First Epistle to the Corinthians.* Grand Rapids: Eerdmans

Fortune, Don and Katie
1978   *Discover Your Motivational Gift. A Depth study of Romans 12:6–8.* Washington, WA: Edmonds

1987   *Discover Your God-Given Gifts.* New York, NY: Chosen Books

1989   *Discover Your Children's Gifts.* New York, NY: Chosen Books

Gee, Donald

1930   *The Ministry-Gifts of Jesus.* Springfield, MO: Gospel Publishers

1972   *Concerning Spiritual Gifts.* First edition 1949. Springfield, MO: Gospel Publishers

Gaffin, Richard B. Jr

1996   "A Cessationist View." in Grudem, Wayne, ed. *Are Miraculous Gifts for Today?* Grand Rapids, MI: Zondervan. 25–64

Glaser, Barney G., and Strauss, Anselm L.

1967   *The Discovery of Grounded Theory: Strategies for Qualitative Research.* Hawthorne, NY: Aldine de Gruyter.

Glaser, Barney G., ed.

1994   *More Grounded Theory: A Reader.* Mill Valley, CA: Sociology Press

Grudem, Wayne

1988   *The Gift of Prophecy in the New Testament and Today.* Westchester, IL: Cross Way

1994   *Systematic Theology. An Introduction to Biblical Doctrine.* Grand Rapids, MI: Zondervan

Grudem, Wayne, ed.

1996   *Are Miraculous Gifts for Today?* Grand Rapids, MI: Zondervan

Guthrie, Donald

1990   *New Testament Introduction.* Downers Grove, IL: InterVarsity

Hagin, Kenneth E.

1981   *Tjenestegavene. Og Gud satte i menigheten: apostel, profet, evangelist, hyrde og lærer.* Norwegian translation by Anne Hove Sunnarvik. Torp, Norway: Livets Ord Forlag

Hallesby, Ole

1924   *AAndens Fylde. Oppbyggelig Foredrag over den Tredje Artikkel.* Oslo: Lutherstiftelsen

Hesselberg, Thor, et. al.

1977   *Dere Skal Få Kraft, Bibelens Tale om Åndens Gjerning,* Oslo: Credo/Luther

Horton, Stanley

1979   *The Holy Spirit; a Study Guide, What the Bible Says about the Holy Spirit.* Brussels, Belgium; International Correspondence Institute

Hummel, Charles E.

1978   *Fire in the Fireplace.* Downers Grove: InterVarsity

1979   *Fire in the Fireplace, Contemporary Charismatic Renewal.* Oxford: Mowbray

Hunter, Todd

1999   *Wimber and Hunter on Spiritual Gifts.* Lecture at "Back to the Basics" conference in the Anaheim Vineyard Christian Fellowship in Anaheim, CA

Hvalvik, Reidar

1988   *Romerbrevet.* Unpublished manuscript. Oslo: Menighetsfakultetet Skrivestua

Jackson, Bill

1999   *The Quest for the Radical Middle: A History of the Vineyard.* Ladysmith, South Africa: Vineyard International Publishing

Jensen, Richard

1975   *Touched by the Spirit.* Minneapolis, MN: Augsburg

Jørgensen, Jens Petter ed.
1977   *Åndens Gjerning i Liv og Tjeneste,* Oslo: Luther

Jørgensen, Jens Petter
1986.   *Mulighetenes Gud, en Enkel Innføring av Hva det Vil Si å Leve et Liv i Ånden,* Oslo: Luther

Kung, Hans
1967   *The Church.* New York, NY: Sheed and Ward

Kvalbein, Hans
1991   "Embete og Nådegaver." In Eikli, G., ed. *Kvinner – i Bibelen – i Kirken – i Misjonen.* Oslo: Luther

Ladd, George Eldon
1974a   *A Theology of The New Testament.* Cambridge: Lutterworth
1974b   *The Presence of the Future.* Grand Rapids, MI: Eerdmans

Mare, W. Harold
1985   "Commentaries to 1 Corinthians " In *The NIV Study Bible.* Grand Rapids, MI: Zondervan

Mitchell, Costa
1999   *Network Manual.* Adapted from original with same title, Bugbee, Bruce, Cousins, Don and Hybels, Bill., Grand Rapids, MI: Zondervan, 1994. Unpublished manuscript used by the Vineyard Churches in South Africa. Hillside Vineyard Christian Fellowship, Johannesburg, South Africa
2001   Personal interview May 23rd, Oslo, Norway

Nathan, Rich
1998   "Bible Teacher." In Pytches, David, *Influence and Legacy.* Guildford, England: Eagle. 95–104.

Nathan, Rich, and K., Wilson

1995   *Empowered Evangelicals, Bringing Together the Best of the Evangelical and the Charismatic Worlds.* Ann Arbor, MI: Servant

Nerheim, Øyvind

2000   *Church Conflict: The Pastoral Overseer's Authority Base in a Relationship Based Church Movement Like the Vineyard.* Master of Theology in Intercultural Studies thesis presented to the School of World Mission at Fuller Theological Seminary in Pasadena, Los Angeles, CA.

O'Connor, Elizabeth

1971   *Eighth Day of Creation: Gifts and Creativity.* Dallas, TX: Word

Olsen, Runar Helge

1989   *Nådegavene – Etterfølgelse i Praksis. En Presentasjon og Vurdering av John Wimber's Teologi, med Særlig Henblikk på hans Nådegavesyn.* Unpublished thesis, Oslo: The Norwegian Lutheran School of Theology

Packer, James, I.

1998   "The Intellectual." In Pytches, David, *His Influence and Legacy.* Guildford, England: Eagle. 257–268.

Prince, Derek

n.d.   "A Explanation of the Greek Word *Charisma*," and "*Charisma* – Genuines and Species." From the lecture tape series; "*The Nine gifts of the Holy Spirit.*" No publisher

Pytches, David

1985   *Spiritual Gifts in the Local Church.* Minneapolis, MI: Bethany House

Pytches, David ed.

1998   *John Wimber: His Influence and Legacy.* Guildford, England: Eagle

Riiser, Sigvart
1970   *Åndsutrustning og Nådegaver.* Oslo, Norway: Lutherstiftelsen

Rue, Brent
1988   *Åndens Gaver (the Gifts of the Spirit).* A compendium to John Wimber's lecture series at the Lutheran charismatic renewal conference "Oase1988" in Gøteborg

Råmundal, Lars
1997   *Skjulte Ressurser, Elementer til en Teologi om Menighetens Oppbygging, Fornyelse og Vekst.* Rex Forlag

Sandnes, Karl Olav
1996   *I Tidens Fylde,* Oslo: Luther

Sannes, Kjell Olav
1991   "Kvinners tjeneste i Kirken." In Eikli, G., ed. *Kvinner – i Bibelen – i Kirken – i Misjonen.* Oslo: Luther

Shaw, Gregg
2002   Personal Interview 8th of May, Oslo, Norway

Sohm, Rudolph
1892   *Kirchenrecht.* Leipzig: no pub.

Sjogren, Steve
1993   *Conspiracy of Kindness.* Ann Arbor, MI: Vine

Skjevesland, Olav
1976   *Jesus Gjerninger og Diakonien,* Diakoni og kirke, Andreas Aarflot ed. Oslo: Luther

Skottene, Ragnar
1980   *Bli Fylt av Ånden!* Oslo: Luther

Spittler, Russel
1976   *The New Pentecostalism: Reflections of an Observer.* Grand Rapids, MI: Baker

Spittler, Russel
  1999   "Paul's First and Second Letters to the Corinthians." Lecture at Fuller Theological seminary. Pasadena, CA

Springer, Kevin, ed.
  1987   *Riding the Third Wave, What comes after renewal?* Hants, UK: Marshall Pickering

Storms, Samuel C.
  1996   "A Third Wave View" In Grudem, Wayne, *Are Miraculous Gifts for Today?* Grand Rapids, MI: Zondervan. 175–223.

Sundberg, Hans
  2002   Personal interview by mail 12th of May, Stockholm, Sweden
  2004   Personal interview by phone 20th of September, Oslo/Stockholm, Sweden

Søvik, Oddvar and Skottene, Ragnar
  1983   *Nådegavene, - Menighetens Arbeidsutrustning*, Oslo: Luther

Tangen, Karl Inge
  1993   *Guds Rike og Kirkens Helbredende Tjeneste, en Presentasjon og Vurdering av John Wimber's Forståelse av Kirkens Helbredende Tjeneste med Vekt på Fysisk Helbredelse.* Unpublished Master thesis, Oslo: The Norwegian Lutheran School of Theology

Tegnander, Oddvar
  1991   *Den Hellige Ånd, Gaver, Tjenester og Frukt.* Oslo: Rex

The Second Vatican Council
  1963   *Acta Syndalia, vol. 2, pars 3.* Rome: Vatican

Turner, Max
  1998   *The Holy Spirit and Spiritual Gifts.* London: Hendrixson "Modern Linguistics and the New Testament." In Green, J.B., ed. *Hearing in the New Testament*, 156–8

Venter, Alexander

2000   *Doing Church: Building from the Bottom Up.* Cape Town, South Africa: Vineyard International Publishing

Wagner Peter C.

1976a   *Your Church can Grow.* Ventura, CA: Regal

1976b   *Your Spiritual Gifts can Help Your Church Grow.* Ventura, CA: Regal

1987   "It wasn't me that pulled the leg." In Springer, Kevin ed., *Riding the Third Wave; What comes after renewal?* Hants, UK: Marshall Pickering. 74–90.

1994   *Your Spiritual Gifts can Help Your Church Grow.* Ventura, CA: Regal

2000   *The New Apostolic Paradigm Churches.* Master level class as Fuller Theological Seminary, Pasadena, CA: Fuller

Williams, J. Rodman

1990   *Renewal Theology: Salvation, the Holy Spirit, and Christian Living. Systematic Theology from a Charismatic Perspective.* Grand Rapids, MI: Zondervan

Wimber, Carol

1999   *John Wimber: The Way it Was.* London: Hodder & Stoughton

Wimber, John

1985a   *Spiritual Gifts Seminar Volume 1.* Anaheim, CA: Vineyard Ministries International

1985b   *Spiritual Gifts Seminar Volume 2.* Anaheim, CA: Vineyard Ministries International

1985c   *Spiritual Gifts Seminar Section 4.* Anaheim, CA: Vineyard Ministries International

1985e   *Spiritual Gifts Seminar.* Video. Anaheim, CA: Vineyard Ministries International

1985d   *Spiritual Gifts Seminar. Tape series.* Anaheim, CA: Vineyard Ministries International

1992   Personal interview with John Wimber, Anaheim, CA

1994 *The Gospel to the Poor: Bible Notes for In-Depth Study.* England: Frontier

1996 *Beyond Intolerance: Calling the Church to Love and Acceptance.* Anaheim, CA: Vineyard Ministries International

1997a *Kingdom Evangelism: Proclaiming the Gospel with Power.* Anaheim, CA: Vineyard Ministries International

1997b *Vineyard Reflections: The Five-Fold Ministry.* Anaheim, CA: The Association of Vineyard Churches

Wimber, John and Kevin Springer

1987 *Power Healing.* San Francisco, CA: Harper&Row

1991 *Power Points.* San Francisco, CA: Harper&Row

1992 *Power Evangelism.* Revised Version. San Francisco, CA: Harper&Row

Wright, Nigel

1995 "The Theology and Methodology of 'Signs and Wonders'." In Smail, Tom, et. al., ed. *Charismatic Renewal,* London: Gospel and Culture, 71–85

Printed in Great Britain
by Amazon

47155224R00118